W9-CSM-346

"If you don't know how to take time out for yourself, *The Self-Nourishment Companion* offers you a variety of delightfully creative suggestions."

—Susan Swartz, newspaper columnist and public radio commentator, Sebastopol, CA

The Self-Nourishment Companion

57 Inspiring Ways to Take Care of Yourself

Matthew McKay, Ph.D.

Catharine Sutker

Kristin Beck

NEW HARBINGER PUBLICATIONS, INC.

Publisher's Note

This publication is designed to provide accurate and authoritative information in regard to the subject matter covered. It is sold with the understanding that the publisher is not engaged in rendering psychological, financial, legal, or other professional services. If expert assistance or counseling is needed, the services of a competent professional should be sought.

Distributed in the U.S.A. by Publishers Group West; in Canada by Raincoast Books; in Great Britain by Airlift Book Company, Ltd.; in South Africa by Real Books, Ltd.; in Australia by Boobook; and in New Zealand by Tandem Press.

Copyright © 2001 by Matthew McKay, Catharine Sutker, and Kristin Beck
New Harbinger Publications, Inc.
5674 Shattuck Avenue
Oakland, CA 94609

Cover design by Poulson/Gluck Designs
Cover photo and interior art by Donna Day/Tony Stone
Edited by Jueli Gastwirth
Book design by Michele Waters

ISBN 1-57224-242-6 Paperback

New Harbinger Publications' Web site address: www.newharbinger.com

03   02   01

10   9   8   7   6   5   4   3   2   1

First printing

For my mother, Louise La Brash.

—MM

For Mike, the love of my life who gives me more nourishment than I ever imagined possible.

—CS

For Louise, the bravest girl.

—KB

Contents

Introduction

The great problem with our North American lifestyle is that we are all rushing headlong through our days. We are focused, productive—but malnourished. We have neither the time, nor many of the skills for nourishing ourselves. *The Self-Nourishment Companion* will teach you new ways to replenish and take care of yourself, many of which will steal no more than a few minutes from your busy life.

We grow up with a script that tells us how to live life. It prioritizes, showing what is important and what is trivial. For most of us, the script requires that our work and our responsibilities toward others must always come first. In so many cases our own needs for emotional balance and well-being come dead last. We end up feeling embarrassed or guilty if we take even a little time to nourish ourselves.

But the problem isn't just our priorities. A lot of what keeps us from nourishing ourselves is that we were never given the tools to do so. Many parents spend hours with their children going over homework, or figuring out how to choose the best college, but they spend no time teaching a child how to soothe herself, how to relax, or how to find the things in life that are uniquely pleasing and delightful. Some parents simply don't know about or value self-nourishment. Others never think to pass on the little tricks they've learned over a lifetime for how they replenish or heal themselves.

This book is an invitation for rebalancing, finding new ways to sweeten your daily dose of life. It's about the joy of small pleasures, taking a moment to see beauty, feeling the lovely ways the world can touch us. It's about using our own resources for imagining, for making, for feeling, for laughing, and for reflecting.

You don't need anything special to try any of these fifty-two self-nourishing experiences. Just a willingness to spend a few minutes taking care of yourself. Just the courage to do something new. And perhaps most importantly, a realization that your well-being counts for something, and that you can feel happier if you have the tools.

We invite you to read this book randomly. Dip in anywhere: front, back, or middle. Try things from different categories of self-nourishment—mental vacations, time-outs, self-awareness, pleasures at home, sensory indulgence, etc. If an exercise works, keep doing it. If it doesn't, forget it and go on to something else. Let your own reactions and feelings be your guide.

Why not start now? This little cornucopia of pleasures is yours to explore. Enjoy!

Part I

At Home

Everything begins at home. Why shouldn't the way you take care of yourself start there, too? Many of us keep everything going around us, while our homes fall apart. How many times have you said you would help someone with a project at their house, while your own projects sit idle? Your home, you've heard it before, is your sanctuary. More precisely, your home is what *you* make it. When you're attending to the details of your home, you're inevitably spending time taking care of yourself.

So, what better place is there than at home to start on your path to self-nourishment? While it definitely is easy to place on the back burner your personal needs at work or at your mother-in-law's house, one place you can really take charge is in your own home. You can create an environment in which you really come "home" to yourself—where you nurture your culinary cravings, submerge yourself into warm, bubbly bathwater, or even begin to connect with your community.

Try not to let the usual strains and nagging requirements that come with any household prevent you from taking care of yourself at least once a week. Any of the following exercises can be accomplished in under an hour, if that's all you can squeeze in. But if you find yourself warming up to the idea of self-nourishment, you may find that you'll have time for two or even three exercises in a week's time. Whatever you choose, most importantly, choose yourself. If you can't do that at home, where on earth can you?

Destination: Your Own Neighborhood

When you leave your house for a little neighborhood exploration, the goal isn't exercise, or taking care of a local errand, or driving your car somewhere. The purpose is to imagine you're a tourist in your own daily world. Consider for a moment how you feel when you're on vacation. You're more open to new experiences, ready for anything and anyone. You're relaxed and patient. Your eyes are open, and you notice and appreciate your surroundings. Now, approach your own block with the same kind of wonderment and notice what happens.

Jason takes walks through his neighborhood every day—to the post office, to the store, or just to get some fresh air. But Jason, who has lived in his neighborhood for a year, hasn't yet connected with his area; he doesn't know any of his neighbors and he hasn't become familiar with the sights. Consequently, he dreams of travel and vacationing so he can experience a sense of awe about some place new. "You don't need to travel to faraway places to experience the refreshing feeling of newness often inspired by traveling. It can be realized right outside your front door."

Set aside two hours on a Saturday morning for some neighborhood touring. When you walk outside your door, focus on what you have passed a million times but never actually noticed: a sign, a mailbox, the molding on a building. What do you smell? Eucalyptus leaves? Night jasmine? Garbage? Pizza? Coffee? Whatever it is, it's an olfactory experience unique to your neighborhood. Let yourself become aware of the smell, knowing that it's part of the sensory experience of your street. Next, take an ambling stroll around the block, admire the trees or the facades of the buildings, look at the sidewalk or lane, and notice the gardens or storefronts.

As a neighborhood tourist, you might be curious about when a particular building was erected, or what inspired a certain sculpture or restaurant's theme. You might find yourself more open, friendlier to passers by, people with whom you share a zip code (and possibly more).

Once you've explored your neighborhood as a day-tripper, you'll arrive home with a new fondness and curiosity about where you live. That feeling feeds into a deep sense of community, a basic contentment that is sure to be a nourishing part of your day. Go ahead—discover the exoticness of your neighborhood! It's free.

Tips for your neighborhood walk:

- Leave your home with just your house keys.
- Don't walk out the door with any particular destination in mind.
- Keep your mind flexible and engaged. Don't try too hard to appreciate your surroundings . . . that can limit your experience significantly.

After your excursion, follow up on the interesting things you discovered. If you found a bookstore close to home that you never knew about, go back and buy a book there. If you met a neighbor who told you about the history of your area, find out more about it.

Frequenting your local cafés, bookstores, or corner markets can become a pleasant ritual. Before you know it, you'll become more familiar with your community. Perhaps you'll uncover a nook or spot that will serve as a special treat whenever you need a refreshing pick-me-up.

Skinny Dipping at Home

For thousands of years, people have indulged in the soothing, healing warmth of taking a steam bath. A hot soak can take the ache out of sore muscles and provide a chance for some reflective alone time. Further, bathing is an eminently accessible activity, you get to be nude, and, best of all, depending on how and where you do it, it's completely free. (An old Finnish proverb refers to the steam sauna as "the medicine of the poor.")

Some enjoyable benefits of a steam bath include: total relaxation of mind and body; reduction in stress; relief for muscle tension and stiff joints; elimination of body toxins; stimulation of circulation; and alleviation of sinus congestion caused by colds, asthma, or allergies. And, like a minispa, regular skinny-dipping in your own bath can keep your skin glowing and youthful.

Unfortunately, many of us resist taking a bath. It can be hard to cordon off that kind of time, it seems like a commitment. Imagine telling a three-year-old that it's bath time. Can you hear the protests? Okay, what if you let that kid pick out all of her bath toys, and add her favorite fragrance and color to her shampoo? Do you think she'd be more interested? What if you told her that immediately following her bath, she'd be able to wrap herself in a fluffy towel and watch her favorite movie? Most of us can still relate to that little three-year-old: the three-year-old within, if you will. What could you say to your inner three-year-old that might entice them to take a hot soak?

Anita, a waitress and mother of three, is very familiar with the wars waged around bath time. Because she spends her entire day catering to the often minute needs of others, she has become a bona fide soaker in the evening. Her bathing ritual, step by step, goes like this:

- Run the water in the tub
- Make a cup of tea
- Light some yummy-smelling candles
- Turn on favorite music

- Add salts to the water
- Grab a magazine and the tea
- Soak for at least half an hour
- Emerge refreshed wrapped in towels
- Engage in some more pampering

Even though bathing is technically cost free, it is just a bit more fun when you've invested a little time and money on some good smelling and feeling bath accoutrements. If you can pay for it, quality is nice. But even if you're on a modest budget, there are ways to treat yourself without breaking the bank. Following are some ideas for expanding the concept of taking a bath:

- *A comfy robe and amply sized towels.* Worshipful bathers make a big deal out of the start-to-finish of a bath. A soft, comfortable robe and some full-coverage towels put the final, swaddling touch on a well-executed bath.

- *Lotions, potions, ablutions.* Some are sticky, some are cold, some are fragrant, some are colorful, and some are hypoallergenic and unscented. Experiment to find what your favorites are.

- *Fun bath toys.* Remember your inner three-year-old? Bath paint, a boat, a terry hand puppet . . . celebrate and make bathing fun.

- *A friend.* If you can both fit in the tub, bathing together can be a nice way to catch up on each other's lives.

- *A magazine or book.* Trashy or otherwise, just try to keep it dry.

- *Public tubbing.* For the brave . . . public bathing is an adventurous spin on the traditional bath (though, depending on your modesty level, it might not be nearly as relaxing).

- *A beverage, cold or hot.* Your choice. (Drunken bathing is not recommended.)

Bathe daily or weekly, on a big budget or a tight one, alone or with a pal; bathing can make you feel wholesome and refreshed, and remind you how simple it can be to take care of yourself in just a half hour or less.

Comfort Foods

What would self-nourishment be without comfort foods? Cold, rainy days soothed by big bowls of hot soup, or lonely days fulfilled by the perfect ice cream cone, or anxious times when you cannot eat to save your life—basically, food usually can be a pretty good indicator of our emotional state. But as, well, *some* of us know, eating for comfort can be unhealthy as well as fulfilling. For instance, there are those of us who have eased the boredom and inner pain of a mundane and tedious job with the never-ending desk drawer of happiness—pretzels, candy, chips, etc.—which really just leaves us feeling a little ill.

Alas, halt! There is an answer—healthy comfort foods. It's true, there are scads of healthy and emotionally satisfying foods that you can *choose* to eat for pleasure as well as survival. Laura, a registered nurse, chose this path: It was amazing—she would show up to work and unload a backpack of comfort foods that everyone could actually drool over—not cringe over. Laura is just one of those women: She's radiant, fit, and has a sweet personality. She'll sail into a room smiling, her hair casually piled up on her head, chewing on a piece of crystallized ginger, and full of energy. So, of course, what everyone wanted to know was, what the hell does she *eat?* Is there something in the water she drinks?

Laura shared her wisdom with the whole third floor of the hospital. The secret was that she doesn't deprive herself of foods she truly loves, she exercises, and she simply does not overindulge. Sigh. There are always these simple truths underlying most profound ponderings. Still, Laura shared three of her top favored comfort foods. Don't hold your breath though, it's food you've probably heard of and have just forgotten how delicious it tastes.

- **Baked apples**. Apples are a great source of quercetin, a phytochemical that fights the free radicals that can cause heart disease and cancer. They're also packed with fiber and fruit sugar, helping digestion and stabilizing blood sugar levels. Buy organic apples, too—you don't need all of those pesticides ruining your good intentions. Baked apples are easy and you can find a recipe in almost any cookbook. Basically, hollow out a few apples and fill them with a variety of spices, such as cinnamon or nutmeg, honey, walnuts, and the like. Bake them uncovered at 350 to 375 degrees for approximately forty-five minutes.

- **Berry salad.** Berries are cancer fighting, fiber-filled, sweet, and beautiful. A bowl of berries topped with some low-fat vanilla yogurt, a touch of honey, and a cup of tea—delicious! This treat can ease a sweet tooth and nutritionally satisfy you. The perfect fixings of comfort food.

- **Something from your childhood that always made you feel safe, good, and cozy.** This of course varies for everyone, but in Laura's family, on the nights when no one had energy to make dinner, they always ate breakfast foods for their evening meal. It was always fun and it made the children feel like they were breaking the rules. Pancakes and scrambled eggs were favored, and there were big heaping bowls of Cream of Wheat with mounds of honey and butter, or hashed brown potatoes and chicken-apple sausages. Food from your childhood can bring back the memories of the fun, playful times you had growing up.

Making Soup

As many of us know, food has the ability to make you feel good—especially soul food. No, not collard greens and corn bread, we're talking about making soup. Warm, nourishing, healthy, homemade soup.

Just the process of making soup can bring you down to earth and make you feel good. Choosing ingredients, cutting vegetables, adding this and that, and tasting along the way is a process that can reawaken good feelings in your heart. Eating homemade soup can bring great delight to those of us who are hungry for something real. The warm complex broth, the rising steam from the simmering pot, and the nutritious smell permeating the air can put anyone back in touch with their deepest self. (And your friends will enjoy eating it, too.)

Sam was tired of eating the same food every day: burritos and burgers. When a friend suggested that he make soup once in a while Sam heated up a can of soup he had in the cupboard. He enjoyed it well enough.

One day, however, when Sam was in the produce market he saw a nice young woman with a book of soup recipes collecting vegetables in her basket. Of course, she caught him looking over her shoulder at her recipe. After one of those awkward conversations two strangers have in a market, Sam loaded up on some basics for making homemade soup. Onions, garlic, carrots, celery, potatoes, some barley or rice, bay leaves, a nice bottle of cooking wine, some bouillon cubes, and a bit of enthusiasm left the market with Sam.

That Sunday afternoon, Sam sautéed onions and garlic in the bottom of a soup pot that his grandmother had given him. After adding a little wine and all the other ingredients, the aroma and smell in the air made him feel cozy, warm, honest, and wholesome. Sam kept adding herbs and spices in between chapters of a mystery novel he had started reading. At last it was ready, and he ate it, carefully savoring his creation.

In the weeks to follow, Sam made it his tradition to cook up a pot of soup on Sunday afternoons. The benefits were enormous: He had delicious homemade soup in the refrigerator for days; the process of cooking gave him pleasure and was constantly evolving; no two soups were ever the same; and he had a consistently good topic for conversation at the produce market. Sam eventually branched out into making a variety of soups. He even brought some to his grandmother who was amply impressed by his newfound culinary talent.

Cooking for the Sake of Cooking

Mason was buried in work. He couldn't even see his daily planner for all the papers and documents on his corporate desk. The cycle would begin first thing in the morning—he'd arrive at work already anxious in anticipation of what was waiting for him. Once there, he would white-knuckle his way through the morning, thinking, "After this cup of coffee, I'll be ready to get down to work." By noon he was sweaty, had had too much caffeine to drink, and was still just staring at the growing mound of work in front of him. This process of nervous avoidance would torture Mason until 5 P.M., at which point he would declare the day a failure. "Tomorrow will be better," he would tell himself. But, of course, the cycle just repeated itself.

One morning, Mason decided that instead of going to work he would call in sick and pull the covers over his head. Laying around, feeling anemic and depressed, Mason headed to the refrigerator for some boredom eating. As he naturally reached for chips, salsa, and a cola, he noticed a couple of carrots and some broccoli on the same shelf. Mason was so bored that he thought even cooking could seem fun. He grabbed a few cloves of garlic and some soy sauce and started chopping. Pretty soon he got into it, focusing on the knife's swift slice through the vegetables. He noticed that it actually had a meditative effect.

The next day at work Mason brought in some leftovers—and because he was privately kind of proud of his meal, he made a point of taking a lunch break. Having eaten substantially, he worked without distraction through the afternoon. The experience was so successful that Mason began shopping for cookbooks and interesting spices during his free time. Not three months later, Mason had found himself a soul-nourishing habit: What started as an antidote to ennui became a positive force in his life. He wasn't cooking for his stomach so much as he was cooking for his brain, heart, and soul.

To regularly make cooking a necessary part of total self-nourishment, try the following:

- *Have a patient heart.* Don't assume you'll be Betty Crocker the first time you put on an apron.
- *Use quality ingredients.* If the recipe calls for butter, don't substitute lard.
- *Take your time.* If you rush yourself, you risk not only ruining your food, but also your chances of falling in love with cooking.
- *Make it a sensually panoramic experience.* Add music, friends, wine, and fun napkins to your culinary experience.

Will cooking your own foods make you a more productive worker? Can the process of food preparation be an antidepressant? Who knows? Taking the time to care for yourself, however, always yields good results. Putting healthy food into your body can lengthen your life span, and experimenting with different colors, aromas, and flavors will add richness to your daily experience. Cooking allows you to do all of this at once.

Vacationing at Home

You've seen them a hundred times—bulleted lists in magazines with prescriptions for easing stress. A popular tip goes something like this: "Turn off the phone for a few hours and read a book." That might be a good trick for eliminating just one of the forty knots from your neck, but, sometimes, you really need more than a three-hour break. If you don't have the time or money to plan an extended vacation, it's time to be creative. You can plan a full-on getaway—right in your own home.

This was the ticket for Paula, a graduate student on a shoestring budget. She knew she couldn't afford to miss school, and going out of town was financially unfeasible for her. She designed the perfect outing, which she renamed "inning." She wanted to start her vacation on Friday after her last class of the week. She geared up for the weekend by doubling up on her studies so she could escape free and clear of intruding school thoughts. Then she went grocery shopping, and bought every one of her favorite foods.

After gathering up all of her food needs for the weekend, Paula checked out several movies, books, and records from the library. Next, she went home and rearranged her surroundings. She put away all work and bills and other reminders of real life. She created new lounging areas in her apartment, and fluffed up familiar ones. She turned off the phone, put away the computer, and got out her best candles.

While she was priming her living space to become her vacation location, she was thinking of all of the things she likes about vacationing. She likes the plane ride because on the plane she has uninterrupted reading time. She likes hotels because she loves the anonymity of being stashed away, safe but still a stranger. She likes taking walks and she likes sleeping in. So with these vacation goals in mind, she crafted the perfect getaway weekend right in her own home.

It's hard at first to think of your busy, often crowded living area as a haven. It's difficult to turn down requests for your time when you're technically going to be home. It requires a real brain shift to reimagine extended, uninterrupted hours or days by yourself in your own home. But if you plan it carefully, it can be an achievement that leaves you refreshed and reconnected with your home and yourself.

For your vacation "inning," keep the following suggestions in mind:

- Don't simply unplug your phone—unplug your life. Turn off the computer, even storing it in the closet if you have to. Get rid of all evidence of work and "real life."

- Purchase something luxurious to enjoy during your vacation at home. Since you're not spending any money on the getaway, splurge on at least one item that makes it feel like a real vacation. Get a great bottle of champagne or some beautiful flowers . . . just one thing can change the vibe in your house and provide the needed mental shift into celebration mode.

- Do hold the line on being unavailable to anything outside your personal solo vacation.

- Accept no visitors; don't even open the mailbox.

- Before doing anything, always ask, "Would I do this on vacation?"

Don't put off a much-needed vacation or try to take care of all your needs in the measly two-weeks allotted to you by your place of employment. You can relax and enjoy a bit of luxury anytime you want—vacationing at home is an easy, inexpensive, and nourishing option.

Part II

Just Indulge

Chances are you were taught the basic rules of life survival as a youth. Many of us were taught to do our homework, finish our chores, and collect a modest allowance. This prepared us for the big bad world of careers and grown-up responsibilities. As an adult, it didn't come as a surprise when we realized we needed to rise in the early morning to the sound of a hideous blaring alarm clock, gulp down a cup of coffee, head off to perform the grown-up chore of work, and collect the grown-up allowance called salary. Before we knew it, this became the meaning of life.

Maybe, but perhaps not.

Many of us may go through the rituals of survival with a deeper sense of something greater, or even something smaller. We may crave spiritual insight, or perhaps we yearn for simple pleasures, such as the time to close our eyes and take in the smells of a flower garden, feel the sun shining warmly on our faces, or to relish the comfort of a cozy oversized robe and a good novel. The truth is, it's never too late to retrain yourself to do your homework, take out the trash, and then receive a massage.

There are simple ways to treat yourself well. You don't need hours, weeks, or an abundance of money. It can be as simple as slipping into a pair of cashmere socks, listening to music, or learning a new relaxation technique. Allow yourself to experiment with the pleasures offered on the following pages. Indulge yourself by prioritizing self-nourishment—everyone benefits when you feel good.

Don't Throw Out the Trash

We all know that quality literature can be satisfying at times, but what about mindless stories, pulpy novels, and fashion magazines? These so-called "guilty reading pleasures" occasionally can prove themselves to be extremely self-nourishing. Sometimes it can feel calming when you let go of your intellect for a bit. Allow yourself to read for *easy* pleasure, whether this includes reading about the lives of rock stars and fantasizing about their riches, or settling down with a juicy mystery novel. The point is you allow yourself to quickly and simply escape pressure-free.

"Trash" defines anything that isn't too difficult to obtain or understand, and ultimately is disposable. It can fall under the rubric of fantasy, if you're truly transported by it. Granted, it can be embarrassing to admit you enjoy this kind of indulgence. Do reruns of the *The Lawrence Welk Show* secretly captivate you, or do you skulk away from the grocery store with a *National Enquirer* newspaper tucked under your arm?

The promise of trashy activities is that they can completely "numb" your brain—or, perhaps on a deeper level, it's that you give yourself permission to not be so on top of it all. You allow yourself to tune out from personal problems and instead absorb yourself in a soap opera or a detective novel, where, comparatively, the plights of the characters are truly epic. You let yourself care, for a short period of time, who's launching a paternity suit against which famous rock star, or about which daytime talk show host is bulimic.

What else can be described as trash? Cara, a bookstore manager from Michigan who defines herself as "intellectually curious," described her trashy indulgences like this: "Let's just say that I was alone, there was music, wine, and candles, and my right wrist is sore today . . ."

Turns out, what Cara was sneaking away to do was indulge in a gothic video game. When she feels overwhelmed by work or she feels she needs a small vacation, Cara retreats to her computer, where she is totally subsumed into cyberspace for about three hours. Mind you, this is the complete opposite of Cara's regular intellectual, mature, "together" self. She says that with most entertainment, she unwittingly figures out a way to turn it into "work." If she likes a particular novelist or film director, for instance, instead of just enjoying herself she feels she needs to slavishly slog through their entire oeuvre, so she can "master" the artist. With a video game, Cara can't turn it into work at all—more precisely, she refuses to.

What's your favorite form of turning off your brain? It could be something deliciously moronic, like *The Three Stooges*. Or it can be something more chilling to the objective observer. Kristin, for example, feels oddly and completely relaxed when she indulges in material that speaks directly to her true-crime fetish. Whatever it is, make sure you remove your guilt hat before you sit down for a guilty pleasure. Clear some time and your conscience and devour the trash.

Getting Away from It All

Sometimes, getting away from it all is the only way to get back in touch with yourself. The next time you need a nurturing return to self, grab a backpack, a map, a bag of granola, and a sturdy pair of boots. Being in the great outdoors with the glory of the natural world surrounding you can provide just the epiphany you need and the life perspective you're missing.

Mike loved the outdoors. He always loved reading about faraway adventure travels, loved to feed the ducks at the lake in the park, and loved watching those nature shows on cable TV.

One weekend he bought an old backpack at a neighbor's garage sale along with a few other odds and ends: a compass, a canteen and water purification kit, and an old book about the local wilderness area. On another day, Mike found himself in the outdoor equipment store. After purchasing a reasonably priced pair of boots and some appropriate food for backpacking, he felt ready to explore the outdoors.

Mike called his old college pals Gwen and Zoey, who he knew had done some treks in faraway places, and they planned a three-day trip for mid June. They left early afternoon, grabbed a greasy dinner along the way, and made it two miles up the trail in the twilight of late spring. Gwen and Zoey pitched the tent while Mike tried to remember what Jack London had written about how not to build a fire.

Sleeping in a borrowed sleeping bag on a foam pad, Mike awoke from a night of nature's calm quiet feeling very faraway and a little less restless than normal. After eating hot cereal, drinking some camp coffee, and doing a few stretching exercises on a sunny rock, they hit the trail.

In the end, Mike really did get away from it all, physically, mentally, and spiritually. No television, no phone calls, no mean bosses, and no loud neighbors to crowd his thoughts. He conquered a mountain, reunited with old friends, and did it inexpensively. Most of all he took the chance to think about his life with the clarity and reflection that perhaps only nature can provide.

If you have never been two or three days walking distance from the nearest form of civilization, then sign up for a group trip or call up an old friend who's experienced in backpacking. If you haven't been backpacking since you were a scout, then dig out that tin mess kit and that weird set of silverware that fits together in one piece. The modern world is still full of places, large and small, close by and far away, that are capable of transporting you into the tranquility of nature. The busyness of your life can melt away, one step at a time, letting your true essence shine in a way your ancestors would envy.

When All Else Fails, Self-Massage

Sean is a baker—he spends all day stirring, mixing, and kneading bread. He would often peer at the mixture of flour, eggs, and sugar in his big bowl, and think, "Damn, these are some lucky ingredients. I wish someone spent the day kneading me like this." He'd come home and ask his girlfriend, Trina to, "Pleeeaaaassse, just give me a five-minute rub!" But Trina spends most of her days teaching third graders, and she's tired in the evenings. She wants a massage too.

Trina and Sean solved their dilemma by buying a few books about self-massage. They quickly took to the hot tubbing and bath suggestions, but even more helpful were the simple self-massage tricks.

The focus of self-massage is to locate and massage pressure points on your body. You apply pressure, firmly but not so as to inflict pain, on muscle areas that seem tender or tight. Massage actually loosens chronically contracted muscle fibers, while also stimulating the blood circulation in these tense muscles and flushing the toxins from tightened muscle fibers. Four techniques that are simple to do are the "finger walk" and the "finger stroke" for your shoulders, a nifty tennis ball technique for the midback, lowerback, buttocks, and hip areas, and using palms and thumbs for the low back and sacrum area. You can do these just about anywhere without being too conspicuous.

1. **The Finger Walk**—Reach your arm across your chest and clasp your shoulder with your hand (as if you're going to scratch a mosquito bite on your shoulder). Using your fore and middle fingertips, firmly walk your fingers across the muscle. Feel for tender spots and gently press on sensitive areas. When an area is particularly painful, pause on that spot, pressing firmly for ten to thirty seconds, until the pain begins to fade. Then, continue your finger walk across the shoulder area.

2. **The Finger Stroke**—Instead of applying direct pressure with your fingertips (as you did in the finger walk), use the pads of your fingers and stroke the tight muscle area. It may be useful to pretend you are brushing sticky dust

off your shoulders. Use a bit of pressure, and, as in the finger walk, search for tight or sore spots. Many medical professionals recommend that massage strokes move toward your heart. That is, you should begin your stroke further away from the center of your body, and end your stroke closer to the center of your body.

3. **The Tennis Ball Rub**—This exercise is useful for easing pain in your midback, lowerback, buttocks, and hip areas. Place a tennis ball or two in the center of a towel or an old pair of panty hose or socks. Put rubber bands on either side to keep the balls in place. Now, lay on the floor with the tennis balls beneath you, moving your body and the tennis balls over your sore areas. If you would prefer to stand, place the contraption between you and a wall, lean against the tennis balls, and massage the sore areas of your body against the tennis ball device. Depending on the degree of soreness you are experiencing, be careful not to lay or lean too heavily against the tennis balls.

4. **The Sacrum Stroke**—To ease lower back pain and loosen up your pelvic area, use the sacrum stroke. First, stand akimbo. That is, stand with your hands on your hips. Place your palms flat against your hipbones, and, using your thumbs, make little circles on the muscles on either side of your spine and across your sacrum area (the triangular bone mass located at the bottom of your spine). If it feels good, move your hands up and down your back massaging along the way. You can reverse your hand position, if it's more comfortable, and use your fingers instead.

A Touch of Decadence

Not many of us have the good fortune to be fluttering around as though we were characters from *The Great Gatsby*. We can't exactly spend our days roaming around in slippers on the Peruvian marble floors, wrapped in furs, wondering who's to host the next gala affair.

That doesn't mean, however, that we can't indulge in our own way. Most of us can squeeze in little activities that can make a difference; we just forget that we can and, sometimes, we are apathetically stuck in old patterns and behaviors. If you're anything like Josephine, you might relate to a childhood of hand-me-downs, the best of JC Penny's clothing from Grandma, and Mom's old ten-speed for recreational use. In college, Josephine learned the art of thrift store shopping and sale racks. As an adult with a modest salary but a nice enough lifestyle, she finally learned how to slip in a touch of decadence now and then. Some may call her a rather talented *creative pleasure seeker*. As the three suggestions below will reveal, there are ways to indulge that will bring ample pleasure for a fair price.

1. **Soaking in Redwood Tubs**—One of Josephine's favorite monthly treats is a trip to the local public hot tubs. The local facility in her area offers clean and peaceful private hot tub retreats for a mere $10 per hour. For an extra $30, she can receive a half-hour massage beforehand. This definitely makes for a pleasurable, soothing evening, and it's simple. You don't have to own a hot tub to go for a soak. Check the "Hot Tub" listings in the yellow pages of your city's phone book, or look in your local weekly paper if you trust their recommendations. These days, there are plenty of respectable, clean massage and hot tub locations. Ask around, maybe your friends already know of a good place to soak.

2. **Cashmere Socks**—Buying and wearing cashmere socks is another of Josephine's favorites. This is just one of the small, everyday pleasures that can add a touch of decadence to your life. When your thinking sweaters, sure, the price alone may tend to keep you away from purchasing cashmere material.

But socks are affordable and comfortable. And don't think, "Oh, cotton socks are just fine." Spend the extra $10 and acquire a pair of divinely soft cashmere socks—you know Daisy would've! Even if your socks end up costing more than the rest of your outfit, amazingly cozy socks always add a touch of sensual pleasure throughout the day.

3. **Fresh Cut Flowers**—Treat yourself to fresh cut flowers at least once a week. A few years ago, her friend Monique permanently altered Josephine's self-nourishment commitments. Monique had had a small argument with her boyfriend, PJ. On the way home from his houseboat, Monique stopped at the corner flower shop and picked up a large bouquet of beautiful hydrangeas, roses, and small forget-me-nots. Monique proceeded to arrange the flowers as soon as she got home, and then made herself a pot of warm cider with mulled spices. Josephine stopped by after a miserable day at work, and, seeing the flowers, asked, "Gee, what's the special occasion?" Monique replied, "Special occasion? I'm the special occasion." Mo didn't see any point in going home to wait by the phone for her boyfriend to call. Instead, she got to work taking care of herself!

   Josephine appreciated Monique's response so much that she has made it a personal tradition to treat herself to a bouquet of flowers once a week. Why do we have the silly idea that someone else needs to buy us flowers? If there's something you know you enjoy, don't wait around for someone else to provide it for you. Brighten up your own life—you deserve it.

You can enjoy the luxuries of life, regardless of your budget or lifestyle. Many of us are so accustomed to refraining and pinching our pennies that we completely forget to treat ourselves once in a while. It's similar to going on a diet for ten years and forgetting that you *can* have a cookie or an ice cream cone now and then. So go for it . . . introduce at least one simple pleasure into your daily life and enjoy yourself.

Learn to Say "No!"

Is your time infinite? Are you one of the lucky people who have more hours in a day than the rest of us have? Is your day spent waiting for the opportunity to serve others—drive children to soccer practice, take care of your mother's bills, shop for dinner, finish two reports for your boss on top of the project you already have going, solve your friends problems, and so on? Is this what you envision for yourself, what you always dreamed of? What did you dream of, anyway?

Unless you have one extremely demanding person in your life who expects you to be everything to them, chances are you have multiple people who only expect a small, itty-bitty portion of your time and energy. No one really thinks about the fact that they are one of many demands on your time. Your best friend thinks, "Hey, I'm your best friend, this is what we do! We discuss our lives and figure it all out together!" While you may be thinking, "I don't care about your life, my life, or anyone else's right now, all I want is food, shelter, and a long night's rest."

People cannot read your mind, however, and they cannot know that you are truly thinking "No!" when you verbally say, "Yes! I'll solve your life, fix the leak in our sink, drive you across town, and shovel snow!" The only person who can communicate "No!" is you, and you can. No one is going to fall apart, spontaneously combust, or walk through a blizzard just because you get assertive once in a while.

Cynthia always used to respond positively to everyone's demands. Then, before she knew it, she'd be at the end of her rope. Suddenly, she'd be irritable, snappy, and aggressive. She'd go straight from being too compliant to request after request, to leaping to the other extreme—aggressive and curt.

Then she would feel guilty, and she couldn't understand why. What Cynthia finally figured out was that she needed to practice saying "No!" more regularly. Learning to recognize your own needs—and to take care of them—is a very important component of self-nourishment. This doesn't mean that you take care of yourself only after you're done taking care of everyone else. Sometimes, you must take care of yourself *first*. So how do you teach an old dog new tricks?

Here's how Cynthia did it. First, she realized she automatically would answer "Yes!" before she even considered if the request was really something she wanted to do. If you relate to Cynthia's automatic "Yes!" response, consider the following suggestions the next time someone asks you for a favor:

1. **Pause**. Don't offer an answer right away

2. **Consider your needs**. Are you about to sacrifice your needs?

3. **Respond**. Provide an honest response that is based on your true assessment.

When Cynthia applied these three steps, her next experience went like this: Her boyfriend asked her, "Hey, can you drive me to the airport tomorrow morning at the crack of dawn?" She **paused** to think about it. Did she truly want to wake up *before* the crack of dawn in order to get him there on time? She **considered her needs**. The morning in question was her one morning to sleep in, and besides, he could actually take the shuttle quite easily. She **responded** truthfully, saying, "No. I do not want to." She offered to pick him up, as his flight came home conveniently at a reasonable time.

The more Cynthia tried this, the better she got at it. Remember to assess requests and demands. People will still love you, even when you say "No!" (And if they don't, their demands aren't deserving of your time anyway.)

Breathe Easy

It's almost silly to realize that we often impede even the most basic physiological response of breathing. We think we're taking care of ourselves—we eat healthy amounts of fruits and vegetables, we jog, we bike, swim, go to therapy, the works. But we forget to breathe. Although it's true, how can this be? Have you ever caught yourself washing dishes or studying a textbook or your tax records and then realized you were holding your breath?

Perhaps you've noticed as you become more nervous about something, or feel anxiety rising in your chest while thinking about some undone task or unpaid bill, your breathing quickens. Instead of taking in deep amounts of oxygen and filling up your lungs to their capacity, you take shallow rapid breaths—kind of like a hummingbird. And I don't know about you, but hummingbirds don't strike me as one of the calmest beasts amongst the animal kingdom. Guess what? It's time to breathe!

Believe it or not, there are numerous schools of breath, so to speak. Different psychologists or physicians, or yogis or gurus, have developed their own techniques. Jon, a committed daytime activist and nighttime bartender, likes to practice the progressive muscle relaxation (PMR) method, created by Edmund Jacobson back in 1929. Here is what longtime follower Jon manages to practice daily:

First, Jon begins by tightening and relaxing large muscle groups in his body sequentially. He tightens each muscle group for seven seconds, and then releases. On the release, he notes what sensation he is experiencing in each part of his body. He questions whether it feels heavy or tingly. With enough practice, Jon explains, he is able to tell the difference between relaxation and muscle tension. Sometimes certain muscles are so chronically tense that they just stay tight and you may believe the feeling is normal. This isn't good. But, by practicing PMR regularly, certain muscles will begin to release some of their built-up tension.

In *The Daily Relaxer*, authors Matthew McKay and Patrick Fanning suggest doing the following PMR sequence:

- Take a deep breath all the way down to your abdomen. As you exhale, let your whole body release into relaxation.
- Clench your fists, arms, and chest muscles. Hold for seven seconds, and then relax. Pay attention to the relaxing sensation you feel in these areas.
- Screw up your face as if you've just sucked on a lemon. Tighten your neck up, too. Hold for seven seconds, and then release. Roll your head around to further loosen up the neck and facial muscles.
- Inhale deeply so that your stomach pooches out. Hold for seven seconds, and then relax. You should feel your back and stomach release some tension.
- Flex your feet and toes. Tighten your buttocks, thigh, and calf muscles. Hold and then release.
- Finally, point your toes, again tighten your buttocks, thigh, and calf muscles. Relax after seven seconds. Now scan your body and feel how the relaxation has spread from your head all the way down to your toes.

Another Way to Look Inside

Throughout our lives, many engaging activities encourage us to ponder life's grander purposes while having a bit of fun. In junior high there is the Ouija board. In high school, we might read newspaper horoscopes and astrology books. In college, Psychology 101 teaches students how Freud, Jung, and maybe some philosophical or existential framework can assist in "understanding it all." Regardless of our age—whether we're twenty-two or 102—the questions of who, why, and how always will intrigue us.

Learning about and playing with the Enneagram is another fascinating, fun means of personal exploration. Thought to have originated in the ancient Sufi tradition, the Enneagram has evolved into a system of human development that maps nine different personality types and their interrelationships into succinct categories. The Enneagram can be an interesting way to gain some insight into your personality type. Of course, to summarize this ancient system would be to oversimplify it, but if you like this kind of thing, playing with the Enneagram can be an engaging way to nourish yourself.

Toby and Jed, who have been close friends since the third grade, and their neighbor Karen, who continually is interested in expanding her personal development, decided to spend an evening exploring the Enneagram. Because they only had a limited amount of time and a couple bottles of wine, they decided to skip learning about theory and history, and instead went straight to reading about the Enneagram's nine personality types, which could provide insight into each of their respective life circumstances.

After perusing the specifics of this beautiful, complex, ancient tradition, Karen found she identified strongly with personality type number two, The Giver. Karen gained new perspective about how she naturally interacted with her father and her sister. Inspired to study the Enneagram more deeply, Karen attained clarity regarding her own needs and expectations in her relationships.

Following are very brief summaries of the nine Enneagram personality types as explained by Tony Schwartz in his book *What Really Matters*. Maybe one will ring true for you.

1. **The Perfectionist Ones**: Often reacting to a history of being severely criticized, Ones try to recover a sense of essential value by attempting to behave perfectly, only to become their severest critics when they inevitably fall short of their ideals.

2. **The Giver Twos**: Rewarded early in life for being pleasing and self-sacrificing, Twos seek affection and approval by putting other people's needs first, but always with the unspoken expectation that they will receive something in return.

3. **The Performer Threes**: Prized as children for their success and accomplishment, Threes come to value achievement and image above all else, and they lose touch with their own underlying feelings and emotional needs.

4. **The Tragic-Romantic Fours**: Beset by a sense of early abandonment and loss, Fours believe that intense, passionate relationships are the key to escaping depression and finding happiness—but forever feel unfulfilled and disappointed.

5. **The Observer Fives**: Intruded on or simply ignored as children, Fives conclude that cultivating detachment and minimizing their personal needs is the surest path to avoid feeling overwhelmed by their own feelings or by the demands of others.

6. **The Fearful Sixes**: Raised by authorities who proved untrustworthy and even humiliating, Sixes conclude that constant vigilance and careful attention to the motives of others is the key to warding off harm and ensuring safety and security.

7. **The Dilettante Sevens**: With an abundance of negative childhood memories, Sevens convert frightening early experiences into selectively happy remem-

brances. They tend to live in an idealized and self-absorbed world, resisting deep commitments and focusing attention instead on all of the possibilities ahead.

8. **The Combative Eights**: Dominated by powerful and demanding people in early life, Eights conclude that the key to feeling safe is controlling others, exerting power, and avoiding any feelings of dependence and vulnerability.

9. **The Mediator Nines**: Overshadowed and often neglected early in life, Nines react by discounting their own needs and merging instead with the agendas of those around them. They tend to resist circumstances only in the passive form.

These summaries are simplified versions of a complex system. If you're compelled to explore the Enneagram further, you will find books on this subject in bookstores or the libraries. Have fun!

It's Easy to Love Yourself

For many of us, thinking about the people in our lives is natural. Not many of us have to consciously remind ourselves to feel love for our children or to wake up and worry about taking care of others. It usually just *happens*. We want to feed them, clothe them, earn money to support them, hug them, pet them, kiss them, wave good-bye to them, and more.

It's usually pretty easy to recognize why we love others: "He's sweet," "She's caring," "He's smart," "She's gorgeous!" "I can always count on her to make swift decisions," "He makes a mean pot of soup!" "I love her beautiful smile!" "He's so nurturing," "She's giving," "He's sharp," "She can name the capitals of each state!" "He never forgets birthdays," or, "I've always loved her strong, capable hands." Take a moment to think of three reasons why you love someone important to you. It wasn't difficult, was it?

Okay, now let's focus on you. How come it's simple to think of loving others, but it's not always so simple to actively love yourself? Make the time to think about you. You can do it. Think about who *you* are. Close your eyes, take a deep breath, and name three *emotional*, *intellectual*, or *psychological* qualities you possess. Take a moment and write these qualities down on paper so that you can visually see positive aspects about yourself that you may tend to forget. For example, when you're with a group of friends, do you usually offer firm suggestions? Do you usually provide practical, useful advice? Are you always on time? Do you always know the answers on *Jeopardy!*? Are you interested in spirituality or politics? Are you creative?

Next, focus on your positive *physical* attributes. We *all* have them, but most of us forget to acknowledge them. For this exercise, lighting candles and dipping into a hot bubble bath can help ease judgmental or critical tendencies. While you're in the bath covered in suds, allow only one part of your body to emerge from the water at a time so that you don't begin your imbedded negative self-talk. Make the effort to look at yourself in a new light.

- Lift an arm out of the water. Notice the suds dripping slowly down your arm, across the crease of your inner elbow area, and over your forearm.

- Enjoy and admire the contour of your wrist and hands. Slowly turn your arm and notice the lines, as if you were observing a sculpture.

- Lightly arch your back so that your belly floats up to the surface, peeking through the thin layer of soapy bubbles. With your finger, move the water around and notice the glistening effect of the candlelight and water on your skin.

- Bend your leg slightly so that your knee emerges. Watch how the water finds its way down your thigh and then disappears and becomes immersed with the bathwater. Your body is sensual . . . enjoy this sensation.

- Close your eyes and allow your head to sink into the water so that your ears are in the bath. Take a few deep breaths and let your body relax. Realize that this is your body, your life, and you can appreciate and relish this truth.

Tend and Befriend

It probably doesn't surprise you to learn that women and men respond differently to stress. It was a 1930s stress study conducted by physiologist Walter Cannon that proposed people have the "fight-or-flight" response to stress. That is, he concluded that our responses to stress are limited to two: we either lash out or run away (i.e., *fight* or *flee*).

A more recent study, however, revealed that many of us—especially women—have developed a more inclusive response to stress due to the fact that we may have dependent young, and therefore choose not to opt to simply fight or flee. Instead, we may have more of a cerebral reaction to stress, which leads us to *tend* and *befriend*. It is calming to *tend* to or nurture others and ourselves. Additionally, many of us have a tendency to *befriend* during stressful times, that is, to rely on the support of a close-knit circle of friends. Often we depend on our support systems to help us through.

Especially during periods of high stress, it's beneficial to engage in simple *tend* and *befriend* activities, such as hanging out on the phone and coddling our young. Why not plan some structured tend and befriend time before stress overwhelms you?

1. **Gardening.** Gardening is a beautiful way to express your creativity, to nurture life, to find peace, and to become centered. In this case, to nurture your tending needs, go for the plants that really require some extra help. Spend a few hours in the morning caring for your neglected houseplants. Pick off old leaves, dust the healthy ones, play some classical music, and, of course, water the poor thirsty foliage. If you have outside plants, do the same, but perhaps spend some time pruning a fruit tree, or pulling up weeds.

2. **Call up an old friend with whom you've been meaning to connect**. Come on, now's your chance! We all have those friends who pop up in our dreams, or into conversations, or into our thoughts when we aren't close to a phone. Make the time to connect with them. Don't worry about offending someone

by trying to explain why you haven't had the chance to call, just call. Most likely your friend will simply be happy to hear from you.

3. **Spend a Saturday morning walking with two of your closest friends**. This shouldn't be too difficult; you just need to make the effort. If you have a family, tell them they have to manage without you for a little while. If you don't have a family, tell your friends they have to ditch theirs. This is important time for friends; we need each other. Not spending precious alone time together can be a sacrifice we don't even realize we're choosing. Make the conscious effort to enjoy the perspective, humor, and energy your friends bring to your life.

Now that we have documented research telling us that humans do well to nurture and be nurtured, we have every right to cuddle up with our domesticated animals and go running to our friends for support when we're feeling stressed. Not that most of us didn't have a sneaking suspicion to begin with, but now it's been proven—we need one another.

Reframing "Downtime"

Sometimes situations in life that appear to be negative actually become positive "time-outs." If you are at home ill, for instance, instead of dreading the setback, you can take advantage of the time and enjoy resting and replenishing your soul. Franchesca changed her strenuous, depleting life routine only after spraining her ankle during a ski trip. Basically, a skiing accident gave Franny her first winter of pure content.

Franny was the Simplicity Movement on the road to a heart attack. She avidly participated in therapy, yoga, exercise, and more. Unfortunately, instead of helping her to feel better, many of these positive activities became other time constraints and stressors. She spent Tuesday afternoons with her therapist, but as the hour came to a close, Franny would literally cut off her highly paid professional midsentence, exclaiming, "Yeah, yeah, okay, got it, so I can't change him. Can I give you my check? I've got to make my yoga class, it starts in about ten minutes."

Spraining her ankle forced Franny into solitude, which was the beginning of a new secret pleasure. Insisting that her partner and all of their friends continue their winter wonderland trip, she found herself at home for a week—quietly alone—with only a novel that she'd lugged around for months, but had never opened.

First, Franny put on her music—the music her children made fun of and that her husband never really liked anyway. She had Carole King, Sarah McLachlan, and lots and lots of Motown hits playing for a week straight. Then Franny made a few minor adjustments to her healthy lifestyle, which incorporated self-absorbed, peaceful, time alone into her winter of content.

1. **Use a prop-pillow**. They sell these things! Franny couldn't stand bunching her comforter into the perfect ball, then turning on her side and trying to fold a pillow in half to prop up the novel she was finally reading. A great invention, prop-pillows allow you to conveniently position books, magazines, or other reading material in a graceful and comfortable manner.

2. **Plant a favorite herb or flower seed and watch it grow.** Franny always fantasized about maintaining a lush, organic, beautiful garden, but the reality of her visions usually turned out a bit on the cruel side. She'd get a whole bed of plants going, and then slowly and painfully, she would kill them all. During her recovery week, however, Franny discovered that if she planted just one item at a time, it was both a joy and a success. She planted some rosemary in one pot, and a gorgeous pink echinacea flower in another.

3. **Add a daily "pure pleasure" item to your to-do list.** Each day that her family was vacationing, Franny would write up a to-do list that included activities she needed to accomplish and at least one item she really wanted to do. One of her lists, for example, read, "Do laundry, buy dish soap, call the electrician, and eat a dark-chocolate, hazelnut candy bar while watching children play in the park."

As her ankle healed, Franny learned the benefits of adding a personal touch to her goals of healthy living—a couple of small but meaningful choices proved to be more powerful than her entire previous collection of self-help habits.

Scents and Sensibility

Going back to the East Coast to visit her grandmother's beach house has always been one of the sweetest experiences of Catharine's life. Nothing compares to the smell of being at the Savannah beach. After hours of travel and anticipation, finally slipping into a pair of flip-flops—one of the pair that has been at the house for the last fifteen years—Catharine heads for the beach. As she walks along the sandy path, she smells the beach instantly: the dunes, the sand and oyster shells that pave the path, the ocean air.

The smells never change and they always elicit the same emotions—peace, playfulness, happiness, and home. Catharine breathes in deeply to intensify the experience. She doesn't know why these smells make her feel so good, but no one has to explain why smelling the ocean, a rose, or the honeysuckle is pleasurable. These things just makes you want to close your eyes and inhale deeply.

Teresa, a centered and patient friend, helped Catharine to realize that she doesn't need to wait once a year to travel three thousand miles to Savannah to experience pure bliss and nostalgia. Catharine, or anyone, can create aromas that make them feel good by using essential oils in a bathtub, on a heated lightbulb, or with a warm, damp cloth.

Aromatherapy uses pure plant essential oils to enhance emotional well-being, and restore your total health in many ways. There are professionals who have mastered the art and science of aromatherapy, but there are also thousands of people who regularly use essential oils simply to feel revitalized and relaxed.

Teresa introduced Catharine to three basic, easy-to-induce relaxation aromatherapy oils. (They may sound a bit like a recipe for spice cake at first, but honestly, these techniques are quite effective.) You can purchase these essential oils at most health food stores, and if not, store personnel should be able tell you where you can. Remember, with essential oils, one drop goes a long way. Test a small area of your skin for possible sensitivity before using the oils more liberally.

1. **Lavender**. This gentle, floral-herbal scented oil has calming, relaxing, and soothing effects. It can be a first aid for stings, sunburns, and muscular aches. It's also a sedative and can help you achieve a deep and restful night's sleep. For a compress, add five to eight drops of the oil to two cups of hot or cold water and mix to disperse the oil. Soak a cotton cloth for a minute or two in the water, wring the cloth, and place on skin. Repeat this every fifteen minutes for up to one hour. Lavender is one of the few oils that you can apply undiluted to your skin.

2. **Sweet Basil**. (Avoid using this essential oil when you're pregnant.) Try using the compress again with the basil oil, or you can add ten to fifteen drops to an already full bath. Basil has a fresh, sweet "green" scent and is a member of the mint family. It has several potent effects: it is uplifting, clarifying, and energizing for stress due to mental overwork, anxiety, and fatigue. It is also a digestion, an antispasmodic, and antirheumatic stimulant.

3. **Ginger.** Ginger has a sharp, spicy scent. It's strengthening for your digestion, fatigue, and muscular aches and pains. It also is an aphrodisiac, antispasmodic, and carminative. Ginger oil can be effective in either a compress or bath, or in a diffuser or nebulizer. Turn on a diffuser for five to fifteen minute intervals; works great as an air disinfectant, too.

Aromatherapy is fun and easy to learn about, and the benefits are soothing, sensuous, and smell good, too.

Soundtracks Induce Fantasy

When we listen to music, most of us would agree that it's a great salve of the soul. Although listening to music is a simple and daily activity, it's sometimes useful and self-nourishing to experience music in a planned and mindful way. Following are three self-nourishing musical suggestions.

1. Make the background music in your life the soundtrack of your mental movie.

   At least four times a week, Natalie, an office worker and mental-escape artist, engages in one type of music fantasy or another. Her repertoire is varied and self-specific. A favorite pastime of hers is driving around aimlessly, pretending that the music in her car is the soundtrack to her imaginary movie. Depending on the tempo or feeling of the song, it could be the breakup scene or the jubilant "I got the job!" scene. It could be the segue from the third act to the finale, or it could be the opening credits, whatever she dreams up.

   When asked about the relative safety issues around using ones car as a vehicle for imagination, Natalie replied, "You're thinking about your bills or your friend or work anyway—why not go the one step further and think about your own movie?" Last year Natalie was immersed in Frank Sinatra's oeuvre, so 'Fly Me to the Moon' was a popular theme song in her mental movie; this year, it's music from Cuba. Natalie hasn't ever been a Rat-packer, nor has she been on Cuban soil, true enough, but luckily, music is so fluid and its interpretations so vast that she can make up whatever she wants.

2. Play the ironic soundtrack game.

   Another favorite musical game is to take a straightforward song and think up the most ironic scene application for it. For example, the decidedly antifeminist anthem "I Enjoy Being a Girl" by Rodgers and Hammerstein could be used hilariously in a movie depicting women taking sweet revenge on a chauvinistic male. That's the game.

3. Listen for individual musical components in multi-instrumented songs.

Another meditative musical activity is listening to music and trying to isolate each instrument used. Normally we hear music as a whole—a body, a wall of sound. It can be incredibly absorbing, however, to really focus on a particular element of the song: bass, drums, guitar, voice, piano, and so on. Sometimes when you're listening for a particular instrument you hear the whole of the music much more efficiently. You can also try to imagine what each musician might look like, what he or she is wearing (are they from the 1940s jazz scene, or are you picturing a nice 1980s punk rocker?). Imagine how the musician appears as he or she strums the stand-up bass, or attacks a drum set. Let you mind wander until you are truly lost in the melody.

You don't have to be a singer to sing, nor do you have to be a musician to take pleasure from this sensual art form. Fantasy and imagination are all you need, maybe a few helpful tips, and there you have it. Take advantage of yet another easily overlooked but invaluable self-nourishment tool—music for the soul.

Part III

Getting Busy

"If you want something done, ask a busy person," so the adage goes. Too often, though, when we think of busyness, we reference commerce with all its trappings. We think of staples and Post-its and documents. We think of office politics or entrepreneurial pursuits. We rarely think of just getting out into the world of possibility, the world of adventure. When this book speaks of being busy, however, it's talking about the importance of honoring your exploratory self, instead of just rushing from here to there without truly experiencing what's happening.

Because most of us are focused on completing our errands, we often believe we don't have enough time for indulgences like planting flowers or candle making or even exercise. Such endeavors, we tell ourselves, are for when we're retired, finished with work, when we have more time on our hands. We're waiting for the children to grow up. We're waiting for our desk to be cleared. We're waiting for the laundry to be folded. We're waiting until the perfect time, the time when every task is completed, every item on the to-do list checked off. We forget so easily that life is one big rotating to-do list, and that just as one list is finished, another begins.

The exercises on the following pages are not designed to make you feel guilty for not getting out there more often. Their main purpose is to show you how easy and infinitely rewarding just adding one self-nourishment activity to your list can be. Perhaps it's about finding some groovy new sport that will increase your heart rate. Maybe it's about taking time just to wander. Whatever it is you choose to experiment with, we guarantee that if you get busy with any of the following suggestions, your to-do lists will become more enjoyable and much easier to conquer.

Restoration

Most of us have aspects of ourselves that desperately need restoration and attention. *Restoration* is the act of returning something to its original state; or it's the restitution of something that has been lost or taken away. Restoration occurs in many forms, in various ways, and for many reasons. Although we may not know exactly what happened to our "original" state or when things began to change, most of us have a sense that there are certain aspects of our deepest self that could use a bit of restorative energy.

Perhaps, for instance, you've lost touch with the kid in you who lived for summer camp, and that playful part of yourself needs a bit of a tune-up. Or your creativity has long been simmering on the back burner of a disconnected stove. Whichever part of you needs restoration, you easily can restore and recharge it.

Leah, for example, works long and intense hours each week as a nurse. Some evenings she feels particularly haggard, after a long shift at the hospital, exerting her efforts for those she loves, cooking for herself night after night, and basically not stopping to take care of herself.

Luckily, Leah realizes when she is in such a state. She knows when she needs to check out of her daily routines and spend some time restoring her energy and zest for life. Even more importantly, she has figured out what kinds of activities replenish her reservoir of spirit. Because she recognizes the need to restore, Leah literally chooses to restore items in her possession. Old furniture she has inherited from her grandmother, gardening tools in need of a good cleansing, sewing or mending a favorite shirt that's been waiting for buttons. Leah always feels productive and satisfied with her labors when she finishes (or refinishes) a job.

To reignite the spark inside of you, try restoring *something*—refinish, polish, clean up, and bring back to life a bicycle, an old piece of furniture, or something else in the storage shed that's been calling for your attention.

- **An old bicycle**. If you have a dusty, old bicycle that needs to be repaired or just simply tuned up, pull it out of the closet and spend the afternoon in silent restoration mode. Maybe it needs a new chain, or perhaps you need to degrease the parts, wipe off the old built-up dirt, polish the metal, and place a brand new coat of grease on the cranks, chain, derailleur, and all of the little nuts and bolts. Enjoy the process and the results. When you're finished, take a deep breath, hop on the bike, and enjoy a refreshing, restorative spin around the block.

- **An old dresser or bookshelf**. Do you have an old bookshelf or piece of furniture you've been lugging around for years, waiting for the perfect rainy day before you strip and refinish it? Well, the truth is you can do it on a sunny day just as well. Head down to the hardware store to buy basic supplies and then hang out in your driveway, backyard, roof, or wherever you have some extra space. All of the wiping, scrubbing, sanding, and maybe even hammering can really do a person good. In fact, in times past, people used to live communally and together do tasks such as these as a way to bond and help each other out.

Sometimes physically exerting yourself with a project that requires your creativity, a little sweat, and intense focus will give you a restorative charge. Even if you have a tendency to neglect your own restoration, now you can devote some extra time to yourself and a lingering household project, which will assist you back to your original state.

No Green Thumb Required

If you are convinced you were born with a killer thumb, the gardener's kiss of death, you may have convinced yourself to stay far from any flora and fauna as an act of kindness. Catharine, for example, spent much of her early twenties going through plants and relationships similarly—they looked good and seemed full of life until they needed something. Water, for instance. Sadly, she would watch her green houseplants (along with her boyfriends) curl up and die for lack of water, or her cactus drown in a pool of excess.

Then, in her thirties, something strange happened. Catharine finally stumbled upon her long-lost soul mate, and he taught her to garden. Two things she was sure would never happen—a boyfriend that worked out and plants that lived. It was beautiful. Eventually, they bought a house together, and Michael declared that they would plant a garden. Catharine offered to first paint, or refinish the floors, or, hell, even rip out the plumbing, but Michael calmly led her to the backyard, handed her a bucket of water, a small shovel, and a bunch of flowers that needed to be put in the ground. A love affair sprung up. She couldn't believe how enriching, fulfilling, and meaningful gardening could be. And easy, too!

Try it. Even if you only have a small plot of dirt and not much sun. Head off to your local nursery and ask for help. Explain what amount of light you have in your gardening area and what consistency your soil is (for instance, is it clay-like, rocky, or sandy, or rich, moist, and tilled?) Keep in mind, you can always buy some soil. Once you have a selection of plants and flowers that are best suited for your soon-to-be garden, head for the yard and create. Gardening is beneficial in many ways:

- **Exercise.** It can be quite the workout tending to your soil, digging, lifting, weeding, shoveling, and so on. Hours pass before you even realize your sweating and breathing, and, most likely, deep in thought or daydreaming about your colorful arrangements. It's much more fun than the Stairmaster!

- **Express your creativity**. You can have a whole tray of yellows, oranges, purples, pink, and whites, and it's up to you to arrange how they will blossom in your garden. It's as if the earth is your canvas, and you get to create the splashes of blue forget-me-nots, or the pink cosmos, or the red climbing rose vine. It's impossible for flower combinations to clash—chances are your ideas will be splendid.

- **Spiritual insight**. Gardening can really remind you of the rhythms of life on this planet: working in the garden, digging in the earth, watching plants bud from seed, grow, die, and then become part of the fertile soil for the next plant. You can witness the cyclical nature of life and death, how they are all part of a system that is connected and interrelated. If you have compost, you can watch your waste become the rich nutrients that feed your garden. Working in this way lends itself to reflection. Let your mind wander and enjoy the gratifying activity of gardening.

My Bed Is My Comfort

Keith Nassan, Berkeley craftsman and cabinetmaker, realized something very important about the bed: We spend too much time in bed not to get more out of it. More comfort, more peace, more pleasure. So he started designing beds to fit the unique needs and lifestyles of his customers.

A bed built for a gourmand, for example, had a built-in refrigerator and cutting board. A professor's bed was surrounded with books, with stained glass positioned to catch the morning sun. A woman who loved textiles had cubbyholes and trays in the headboard for knitting tools and yarns. She also had a whirlpool footbath and, for good measure, a tanning lamp. Some beds were sheltered from the world with curtains, some had scrumptious music systems or lovely sconces for candles. All had the height adjusted to each person's taste (as well as sexual interests).

The point, Keith said, was to make the bed a nurturing place. Not just a mattress and springs, but a haven in which to let go and take care of yourself. While few people have the coin for a custom-made bed, it's still possible to find new ways to make your bed nurturing.

- **The Mattress**. First, start with the mattress. For years, Matt slept on a mattress with more ridges than a relief map. When one of his elderly clients declared, "My bed is my comfort," he thought that only applied to the old or the ill. Big mistake. Your bed *must* support you comfortably. Irritability, physical tension, and lost sleep are the price paid. Make it a high priority to find a mattress that's right for your body.

- **Room for your stuff**. The next step is making sure you have what you need by your bed—without getting up. Matt used to have a nightstand the size of a postage stamp. There literally wasn't room for a book and a glass of water. Another error. You need space for everything you enjoy. Shelves for books, papers, CDs; cubbies for projects; space for a phone, for beverages, for exercise weights—anything you'd like to have in reach. Start small. Experiment with a few stackable bins, then see where you want to go from there.

- **Light**. Your bed should be positioned near a good source of natural light. It may seem silly to worry about sunlight in a bedroom, but millions of people suffer from Seasonal Affective Disorder because they aren't exposed to enough morning light. Don't use overhead lighting in your bedroom. Instead, make sure you have a focused light for reading and alternative soft lighting (candles or small shaded lamps) for mood.

- **Temperature**. Nothing destroys comfort more than being too cold or too hot. If you have air conditioning nowhere else, make sure it's in your bedroom. Also make sure you have a heater that's responsive and keeps a constant temperature.

- **Colors and textures**. Colors and textures are crucial to self-nourishment. Select color accents for your bedroom that give you a feeling of peace. Houseplants work well for this. Make sure things don't clash, or just get thrown in your bedroom because you don't know what else to do with them. Also make sure your sheets and your blankets or comforter feel good to the touch. Whatever your skin likes next to it should be abundant in and around your bed. Conversely, if your feet don't like what they touch when they hit the floor, change it. If you've got a spread that looks good but feels lousy, give it to your aunt.

- **Emotional space**. Since your bed is your haven, remove all reminders of tension, confusion, or struggle away from that area. Make emotional space for yourself. If there's clutter, move or cover it. Place difficult or timeline-oriented work in another room.

Your bed has one real purpose—taking care of you. We suggest changing one thing each week to help it do just that.

Getting Crafty

There are those people who are crafty, who spend hours beading beautiful intricate necklaces, create their own greeting cards for each holiday, weave the throw rugs in the front hall that we all thought were imported, or design tattoos.

And then there are those of us who *wish* we were crafty. We look to our friends who bring us gifts at work spontaneously, "Look! Look what I whipped up for you last night! Just something I threw together while watching reruns of *Seinfeld*." And she's handing to her coworker some insanely small and detailed, personalized pet tag for the cat. The tragic thing is that we—the collective we who can relate to the wannabe crafty group—*feel* creative, we even remember a time in our lives when we *were* creative.

What follows is a Greatest Hits list compiled by a group of currently creative crafty buddies. Sometimes all you need to inspire a little creativity is a muse . . . or, if that doesn't work, a "borrowed" idea is nice, too.

Don likes to have potted plants in his house, but pots can really be expensive and often ugly. So Don suggests the following: In most hardware stores you can pick up two or three clay pots, the plain terracotta-colored pots that are relatively inexpensive. Next, head for the arts and crafts aisle and choose some water-resistant paints or tempera. Buy various colors and decorate the pots to your taste. You can paint the top rim one color, like a bright green or blue, and the base another color. They can even clash. It's a great little addition for any room.

Another creative friend, Julia, likes to visit the most multicultural area in her town. The neighborhood is rich in culture and filled with fun art project goodies. There are Mexican shops loaded with piñatas, candy chili-powdered lollipops, and Mexican charms galore. At the Salvation Army, she picked up an antique birdcage. She had no idea why at first, but ended up taking it home and fixing it up; a little paint, a new bottom, and the thing was adorable. It gave her house a neat, antique look that was kind of original. (As long as she didn't start throwing all of her old bills in there. . . .)

Another suggestion is to muster up one of your old picture frames, preferably a plain wood one. If you like the picture currently in the frame, fine, but temporarily take it out. Identify at least two to three colors in the print/picture that you can use to enhance the frame. Get a hold of some paint and try painting the frame one solid color that picks up a certain tone in the photo. Or, paint the frame one solid color, and then add small, randomly placed dots. (White dots can look pretty cute on a solid paint job . . .)

These are just a few ideas to get you back into crafty habits, but the possibilities are endless once you allow yourself the time and freedom to be creative.

Let the Spirit Move You

Any physical movement, that is, moving your body physically, allowing your muscles to stretch and your heart rate to increase, can boost your emotional and spiritual well-being. It's true. Kate F. Hays, psychologist and author of *Working It Out: Using Exercise in Psychotherapy*, reports "The persistence of physical activity strengthens intrapsychic endurance. Rhythmic routine soothes and smoothes our thought. The unification of mind and body connects us with ourselves."

Anna, a yoga instructor and avid cyclist, says that when she exercises, she is able to resolve and work out different conflicts, concerns, and crises in a totally different way. Instead of her usual sedentary and intellectual attempt to access and understand conflicting emotions, exercise encourages her mind to let go and relax, and resolutions begin to emerge on their own.

Exercise doesn't always have to be the image you see in sports advertisements: You don't have to wear the perfectly coordinated, latest high-tech, NASA-tested, wick-away-the-sweat fabric; you don't already have to already possess buns o' steel and abdominal muscles that could stop a speeding commuter train. You just have to have feet and a front door. Walk out of the door with thirty minutes to play, and you'll be on your way.

Anna's personal philosophy is that even if you feel like a lump of Cream of Wheat, and have zero motivation, try exercising anyway. Whatever you do during your half hour will be better and more effective than sitting on the couch. Hays identifies three categories of exercise benefits: physical effects, general emotional well-being and spirituality, and mental and cognitive effects. Exercising also boosts your self-esteem and you most likely will feel more alive and mentally clear.

One effective way to move more is by transforming a few of your daily habits. For example, taking quick, five-minute jaunts up the stairs instead of using the elevator is beneficial; and parking at the far end of a parking lot and walking to your destination makes a difference, too. Following are four additional suggestions:

- **Walk instead of drive**. Instead of driving the mile to your local market, put on your backpack and walk. One mile each way, plus trucking around the store and carrying your groceries back home—it sure beats climbing a Stairmaster for twenty minutes.

- **Plan a Saturday morning hike ritual with your friends**. Exercising with friends always makes it more fun. You'll feel more motivated to spend the morning being physical when you're hanging out with friends sharing stories.

- **Walk the dog**. Take a walk with your dog or offer to walk a friend's canine companion. Take Spot a little farther than you normally would—an extra block or two could add up to ten blocks or more a week.

- **Take a dance class**. Dance is another fun way to exercise and it isn't something you'll dread doing. Funk, Jazzercise, Afro-Cuban dance, salsa, there are many choices, all great for your heart and your booty.

Whatever you choose, remember that every type of movement is better than not moving at all. Start simple and see where your spirit takes you.

Just Bummin' Around

You don't have to wait for misery to come knocking before you slow down and spoil yourself. This is a common pitfall for many of us, and we rarely realize it's a pattern. Obviously there are people who manage to live life otherwise, but they've always baffled those of us rushing around. You know, you double-park on your way to work, run into the café to grab a latte and the paper, and you notice the people who are *just hanging out*. They're adults, they don't look like millionaires, and they don't look homeless. You wonder who they are. Then, you're back in your car speeding down the street trying to lose the parking attendant in her golf cart who's on your tail.

Now it's lunchtime. Perhaps you stop by the same café to grab your afternoon coffee so you can work through dinner, and by God, they're still there. The adults who linger, meet other adults, and join in lengthy conversations about politics, Hegel, film, and the crimes of evil capitalist society. Still perplexed, you head back to work, trying to make a buck, in the vain hope that one day you too will have hours and hours to linger.

But really, how many sick days do you always have left over at the end of the year? If you *had* to have your wisdom teeth pulled, you would *have* to take the day off, wouldn't you? Or say, your cat suddenly had a third eye growing smack in the middle of his forehead one morning, you would *have* to take him to the vet, right? So don't wait for these oddities and miseries, just do it. Take a morning off, midweek, and don't go to the doctor or to the vet or to visit your child's principal. Johnny hasn't beaten any other kids up this week, and your teeth are under control. Just choose to be a bum for the day.

Start off the morning *hanging out* at the coffee shop. Most cities in this glorious country have at least one, but if you're far from a coffeehouse, choose another establishment in which to leisurely *linger*. This is your assignment—relax, and pretend you are one of the adults who subsist on conversation and aimless ambling.

Christina is a copyeditor who makes time for bumming at least once every three months. She tries to find a bench with direct sun that can pound down and warm her back as she reads the paper. Not just the depressing headlines, but the local section, discovering what is happening in her community. Once she stumbled on an article about a local group of women who get together to do community service projects. Christina got in touch with the group, and now spends one Saturday a month working with at-risk teen-agers. Sometimes they'll take the teens out for a hike, or spend the day working on the halfway house where they live. Christina receives great pleasure from her philanthropic efforts.

Perhaps you too will read about a group or organization you'd be interested in joining, or spot an ad for an Indian-food cooking class and finally decide to sign up, or you might just read the comics while you enjoy a morning of smiling, talking with other café patrons, and watching the birds fly overhead. You see, allowing for free, unadulterated time not only makes you feel good, but also can open up possibilities you may not have thought of otherwise.

Cleaning for the Soul

It's possible to clean in a way that is quite nourishing and, in fact, feels *cleansing*. Cleaning? For the soul? Absolutely.

Have you ever felt that your clutter is a reflection of the state of your life? You're so strung out in other ways that you believe you just don't have time to straighten up the piles of mail, launder the small mountains of clothing hiding on the floor next to the dresser, or wash the coffee cups strewn throughout the house? Before you know it, you may start to feel badly about yourself for not getting around to it and, on top of that, you're living space becomes a stressor.

Your home, as you already know, should be your sanctuary. Whether you live in a tiny studio or in a huge four-bedroom house with your family, your home should be a place in which you are surrounded by comfort. It's a place to reflect your personal taste, experiment with colors you are drawn to, or hang exotic textiles that allow you to daydream of faraway lands. But when you come home to a kitchen you're trying to avoid like your in-laws or an ex-boyfriend, how are you going to enjoy a peaceful dining experience?

Jason remembers his mother, Mary, working for a law firm when he was growing up. She would go on business trips that would take her away from the house for weeks at a time. She'd come home and spend half a day cleaning as a way to reconnect with her home. Luckily, Jason and his father kept the basics clean—dishes, food, and clothes were washed, eaten, or in the hamper. But Mary would come home and clean grime that no one else saw. She saw areas that were special to her alone—on one else seemed to mind that the rocking chair had Sunday's paper piled on it

First, Mary would not only wash the dishes, enjoying the warm water and suds, but then she would wipe down the counters and water from around the sink. It was satisfying to her and maybe her alone, but that was the point. After spending just a half hour in the kitchen, she would finish by placing a vase of flowers from her garden on the table. The smell of fresh flowers always made her feel that she was home again.

Next Mary would put on her favorite Mozart CD and spend some time ironing all of her blouses for the week, humming and relishing the physical motions of ironing, a task that always calmed her. As she hung up her freshly ironed work clothes in the closet, she felt organized and prepared for the coming workweek. Then she would change the sheets, fluff pillows, open windows, and burn some incense to clear out the stale air.

When she was finished, Mary would feel relaxed and cleansed. Hotels, courtrooms, and airplanes were completely cleansed from her system. She would settle into her big reclining chair with a book and admire her old oil paintings, the photographs of her family, and the smells of her flowers, candles, and incense. She was home.

The important element to cleaning for nourishment is cleaning an area, chair, or desk that holds significance for you. A space that allows *you* to feel more relaxed and at peace.

Vista Gazing

James Herriot, the veterinarian who wrote so beautifully about life on the English dales, had a favorite vista. It required grinding up a one-lane road in the high country above Darrowby—no small effort. But the view was so rewarding that he paused there scores of times each year, always taking a long moment to "stand and stare."

From that high hill, Herriot could see the patchwork fields on the Plain of York, and the ragged moorlands stretching in the distance. Each time he went, the scene was calmingly familiar and forever changing. Some days he watched cloud shadows mottle the plain, or high cumulus thrusting above the Hambleton Hills. The fields were dark at plowing time, yellow and orange in the fall. The moor turned white by Christmastime.

Always different; always the same. That's the essence of a nourishing vista. It's a place to look out on the world and let go. Everything is far away and small. Everything's as it should be. The light, the sky, the feel of the air changes. The landscape is touched by the hour and the seasons. But the shapes and contours, the essence of the scenes remains comforting and peaceful.

When Matt lived in San Francisco, his favorite vista was on Twin Peaks. He'd sit in the grass, a little down from the road, and watch the Bay darken. He'd see the lights come on at the Ferry Building and the docks. And on Potrero Hill, where his grandfather once owned a speakeasy. Market Street became a steam of white and red as the cars turned on their lights. Then Matt would look across the water to the bright-lit face of the Claremont Hotel in Oakland. Something about the black Bay, surrounded by city lights, was deeply relaxing. His mind slowed, he felt the tension draining from his body.

A vista has special relaxing qualities because:

- You feel above it all, untouched.

- The sheer distance from everything tends to turn off analytical and worry thoughts.

- Your eyes relax, sweeping the panorama rather than studying a particular object.
- There is nothing to do but watch, and experience a growing calmness.
- You are more aware of sky and light, the immutable sources of beauty.

If you already know where a calming vista is, schedule time to visit it each week. Ideally, it could be on the way home from work. Or a road you travel often. It shouldn't be too difficult to get to. If you don't have much time, stop anyway. Five minutes at a favorite vista can be as healing as an hour massage.

If you can't think of a calming vista, this might be a good time to scout one out. It should be a place you can feel the air and see a large expanse of sky—high enough to have a view, but nothing that sets off acrophobia. It should feel beautiful; the colors, shapes, and visual textures need to satisfy you. Most of all, it needs to seem detached from the world and all its daily struggles.

This week find your vista. Go there. You'll like how it makes you feel.

Relish the Routine

Often we believe that if activities, responsibilities, and even relationships aren't *new* they should be disposed of; we may be convinced that if we're not seeking out novelty around every corner, we're living a slow and boring existence. This isn't always true. There's a joy in routine, a comfort in knowing, point by point, what you can expect from a given series of events.

Garth, for example, like any other harried resident of a cosmopolitan city, goes into a reverie about his routine when asked what he does at the end of a hard day. "I go to this Chinese place on Sixth Avenue and order a steaming bowl of roast pork and dumpling soup. I walk across the street and buy a magazine at the kiosk. Then I walk north about nine blocks to my favorite used CD store. There, I allow myself to buy up to, but not always, three CDs of some combination of jazz, punk rock, and classical. Then it's two blocks more to Old Town Bar where there are beers waiting, and, hopefully, a sports game, a spot at the bar, and perhaps my best friend. If no friend, I turn to the magazine. Then it's return to home, where I put the CDs on, and open up a book and read until bed." He loves the sameness of it. As he anticipates each new leg in the journey, he becomes more and more relaxed, putting all the pieces together until he's safely ensconced in bed.

Julie likes to hop into her convertible and methodically drive over each of the four bridges in her area. While there are a few unknown quotients, like traffic flow or whether she has to stop for gas, the whole loop usually takes two hours. As she approaches the first bridge, her mind is still reeling, and her body is wound up tight, her jaw violently chomping on a wad of gum. By the second, she starts to soften, spits out her gum, and turns on the radio, still gripping the steering wheel. When she reaches the third bridge, she's noticing how the breeze whips her hair around, flicking and tickling her neck, and she starts to giggle. As the fourth bridge is crossed, Julie is fully relaxed and taking the air into her lungs deeply, having used the routine of bridge driving as a successfully transcendental process.

Your personal routines might be elaborate journeys, or they might be very simple, like always going to the same park bench on your way home from work. Acknowledge the routines of your life and be grateful for them. Just knowing what's around the corner can be a relief.

A Space of Your Own

For more than ten years, Sarah's husband played basketball every Monday night. At first, Sarah used the time to take care of bills, do the family laundry, and generally take care of the household. Sometimes her son would need help with his homework; on other nights, she'd end up spending hours on the phone counseling her friends with their troubles. It never occurred to Sarah to make this an evening of her own.

One Monday night Sarah looked around and realized, "I have free time!" There was one room in her house that had always been in flux. There were a couple of bikes in it, a table with old, untouched art supplies, a futon for guests, and the litter box. Sarah ended up in this room, intending to clean out the litter box, but something came over. She had a sort of stream of consciousness, only physically. She started clearing out the room, without quite realizing why or what she was doing.

First, the litter box got moved. She stuck it on the back porch and showed their cat, Birdy, where his new bathroom was. Then she moved the bikes into the basement. She knew her husband would protest having to share his basement workshop with the bikes, but Sarah decided, fair is fair. "It's time for me to have this space!" She left the family art supplies in the room, but dragged in an old bookcase to stack it all up on.

Sarah changed three things about the room so that she was surrounded with a space of her own.

1. **Paint**. First, Sarah painted the trim a new color, a bright color that livened up the room and gave it some new energy. She didn't ask anyone's opinion, she just picked out a sage blue that she loved, and gave the cream room a sage-blue lining.

2. **Add artwork**. Next, Sarah moved her favorite Edward Hopper print from the hallway into the room. It's important to have a piece of art to gaze at. When you're writing in a journal, or writing a letter, or sewing, or whatever, and get to a point where you're not exactly sure what you're next move will be,

stop and admire the creativity of a genius. It's often inspiring and can loosen up your blocked momentum.

3. **Add a personal item or two**. Sarah bought a new quilt for the futon. Sometimes, Sarah realized she felt like finishing her Monday nights off by spending the night in the guest bed, alone. She explained to her husband that it didn't mean she was angry, just that she wanted to stretch out, roll over as many times as she needed, or simply drift off to sleep without the other bedside lamp on. Sleeping under the new quilt reminded Sarah of her years of living alone, in a different bed, with a different life. And Tuesdays when she went back to her married bed, she felt a little excited, and apparently so did her husband!

Even if you don't have a whole room, try creating some space in your home that you can claim as your own. You can do something as simple as moving the litter box onto the porch and using the newly cleared corner for your art supplies trunk. A special bookshelf, an abandoned corner of the guestroom, or a storage area all can be transformed with little effort and will provide you with an abundance of solitude and enjoyment.

Room to Grow

Our ability to grow and move is often reflected in our living space. It makes perfect sense—in many respects our home becomes an outward representation of our inner selves.

Livia is a good example. Livia's house is her problem. She is a voracious packrat; she won't hesitate to buy, say, another key chain, even though she will never have enough keys to fill all of the ones she already has. And she's a comfort junkie. She wants to be able to remote control everything from her fluffy bed. She uses her home as a means of distraction—whether it's her constant TV viewing or her rigid need for that third cup of cocoa every evening, she has created structures and routines to manage her emotions. Because her need for comfort eliminates any self-reflection, she experiences an underlying feeling of stagnation and emptiness.

If you're interested in experimenting with how your levels of emotions are mediated by your surroundings, spend time in each room in your house, surveying your surroundings. Focus on the following questions:

- Has anything fallen apart or expired? (Does your pillow leak feathers? Is one of your plants dead beyond resuscitation?)

- Is your house set up as a den of distraction? (Is the TV the most prominent feature of the living room or the bedroom?)

- Is anything unsafe? (Do you keep your flammable blanket next to your heater?)

- Does anything conjure bad feelings? (Does artwork from past lovers hang on the wall? Are you still using the blanket your estranged mother gave you?)

- Do you hate the look of any room? (Notice the wall paint, furniture configuration, and/or clutter.)

- How does it feel to move from one side of the room to the other? (Are there barriers in your way?)

Once you're finished making mental notes regarding your environment, it's time to begin the process of emotionally intelligent interior design. The first step is to get rid of clutter: Make piles of all those scraps of paper—classify them as either recycling or important for filing. Then, look at what needs to be cleared out completely: dead plants; broken furniture which you have no intention of fixing, even if it was your grandmother's; clothing you hate or don't fit into anymore; books you read and didn't enjoy; and so on. It's time to remove that dead weight out of your life.

Next, focus on the furniture. Move pictures, rearrange chairs and couches, turn your living room into your dining room, and switch your bedroom and your office space, if it makes sense. In the process, continue to go through all of your belongings, paying attention to the above questions. You might find that you actually want your living room to be TV-free, or that you can finally let go of twenty years of holiday cards. When you're finished, you'll have a renewed esteem about your home, and it will be safer and more functional—emotionally and physically.

Into the Green

John Muir, the great naturalist who was instrumental in creating Yosemite National Park, craved the beauty of mountains and trees. He came to California to find it. But when his steamer arrived in San Francisco, he witnessed a city still teeming with energy from the gold rush.

San Francisco in the 1860s was a place of limitless possibilities. Levi Straus, for example, never made it as a miner. Instead, he built a clothing empire selling indestructible canvas pants to the men in the gold fields. The transcontinental railroad had just been completed, and fortunes were being made as people poured into the state—needing everything from ranch eggs to Winchester rifles.

Muir was unimpressed. On his first day in San Francisco he inquired about the nearest way out of town. "But where do you want to go?" asked the stranger he'd turned to. Muir replied: "To anyplace that is wild." The man was startled. "He seemed to fear I might be crazy," Muir wrote in his diary.

But it isn't crazy to seek escape from the crush of city life. Quite the opposite. A desire for things green, for the natural beauty of forest, stream, or meadow is something you need to honor. Those who live an urban life endure a setting that's alien to our biology and basic wiring. Concrete and glass are not our natural environment. Our lungs are not made to breathe exhaust. And few of us are inclined to lie down on some asphalt to watch the sky.

That's why we all need to get into the green. Not just your back lawn or a strip of park between buildings. You need a place where everywhere you look you see growing things. Trees or fields or sedge-lined river banks.

Here's what happens to your body and mind when you nurture yourself with the green:

- Physical tension eases—particularly in the abdomen that may chronically tighten in preparation for fight-or-flight.

- Your blood pressure goes down.

- Your city sense of being on guard and vigilant begins to let go.

- Your respiration rate often slows, and your breathing deepens.
- Your sense of time and time urgency becomes less rigid. Nature operates on a different schedule—of light and dark, warmth and coolness.
- If you wait—and pay attention—something happens to your spirit. A sense grows of being part of forest or field. A connection forms to the earth, its creatures and cycles.
- You feel peace.

Get into the green at least once a week. Find places that don't wear you out getting there. Make sure you aren't looking at buildings and cars—just nature. Be certain that you are physically comfortable, that there's a place to lie or sit, and without a load of bugs to drive you crazy. Try to make sure that city sounds don't intrude—you don't want to hear the rush of freeways or a construction jackhammer in an otherwise relaxing meadow.

Make a conscious effort to "let the green in." Don't spend all your time lost in conversation or overactivity. Try to have periods of stillness that open you to deep relaxation and emotional tranquility. Listen to the wind in the branches; watch it riffling through the grass. Feel the air on your skin, smell the musky fragrance of a river bank. Watch the leaves flicker—shadow and light, shadow and light.

Years ago, when Matt had a camper, he liked to drive into Golden Gate Park on Sunday mornings. He always stopped at Spreckles Lake and fixed a little breakfast on his Coleman stove. Then he'd sit in the grass, eating scrambled eggs on a paper plate, watching the ducks navigate among the cattails. Pine, cypress, and eucalyptus leaned over the water; bullrushes swayed with the ripples. Each shade of green formed a note in the harmony; peaceful and restoring. The eggs weren't bad, either.

Part IV

Mental Vacations

You're sitting at your desk as a teen while the teacher rambles on about the Pythagorean theorem. The fluorescent lights are sucking all of the vitamins out of your body. The student next to you is starting to snore as sweater tracks start imprinting on his face. Suddenly, you're transported to a pleasant spot on a hill, kite in hand, and the cool wind whips your clothes around. It's a bright but blustery day here on the hill, and you're about to launch your kite into motion when . . . "Huh?" Your name is being called for the third time, and the impatient teacher demands to know where you've been for the past fifteen minutes. You can't tell her that you've been on a mental vacation, but that's the truth of it. You wipe the drool from your chin and pretend to get up to speed, the ghost of the kite string still in your hand.

Mental vacations such as these didn't stop when we graduated high school. They continue, in various forms, throughout our entire lives. What happens when you take a mental vacation? First, you enter a sort of trance, a meditative state that slows your body down for a nice rest. Second, you allow your mind do what it longs to . . . create little stories, go places your earth-bound body can't, etc. The beautiful result is that mental vacations are simultaneously creative and restful.

The stories and exercises in this section take a different view on daydreaming than your geometry teacher had: Mental vacations are healthy, and, yes, *nourishing*. Treat yourself to a mindful morning, a great joke, a day of confidence, or a quiet meditation. It's time to take a mental vacation, so turn the page, and get packing!

Have a Mindful Morning

Mindfulness is the act of being present, fully awake, and aware. You can attain mindfulness during any task, including washing dishes, drinking tea, answering the telephone, chewing your food, etc. When you are washing dishes, for example, you do it purely for the sake of washing the dishes. You are aware of your breath and you're conscious of your hands under the running water. Your purpose is not to wash the dishes because you want that bowl of ice cream once you're finished. When you are conscious and mindful, you do not live in the future; instead, you live in the present, the *here and now*.

Ester read about mindfulness years ago in college. She'd perused the teachings of the Vietnamese monk Thich Nhat Hanh, and, at the time, really gave mindfulness a go. Instead of flooring her little Honda from fifteen mph to thirty-five mph in five minutes, attempting to cross the tracks and beat an approaching train, she took to slowing down for the loud, clanging bell. She would think, "That Vietnamese monk wouldn't have felt it was necessary to arrive at the market a full two minutes earlier than planned." She would sit patiently at the tracks and remain fully aware: aware of her breath, aware of her hands on the steering wheel, aware that she was alive and in the moment.

Ten years later, however, Ester found herself downing two shots of espresso, thinking, I am missing out. What's the point of all of this if I don't stop for a moment and notice my own life?"

Ester decided it was time to return to the basics of mindful living. She dedicated herself for a week to practicing mindful mornings. Instead of living in a blur, she began to appreciate small and meaningful activities, such as stopping to notice her cat's sweet, striped face or experiencing the pleasure of folding laundry. Ester felt revitalized, more at peace, more alive.

To begin your day mindfully, follow these three simple suggestions:

- **Breathe**. Wake up and pause. Become aware that you are lying in bed. Notice your blankets resting softly on you. Focus on your breath. Don't think.

Breathe in the morning with awareness. Take fifty deep, mindful breaths. Beginning at the number fifty, count down to zero. For each number, fully inhale and exhale.

- **Mindful morning rituals**. Whichever activities you do each morning, perform them mindfully. As you walk to the bathroom, for example, notice how the floor feels beneath your feet. Or, as you brush your teeth, feel the bristles against your gums, taste the toothpaste, etc. Try not to become distracted by outside thoughts or actions. As soon as your mind begins drifting (which it *will* do), simply notice your thoughts, and then let them go.

- **Eat a Mindful Breakfast**. Begin your breakfast with some warm herbal tea. (Caffeine will immediately send your body into a state of anxiety.) Notice the water as it pours from the teapot as if it were a small waterfall. Make sure to sit down with your breakfast. Sip your tea, enjoy its warmth, bite into a piece of toast savoring the wheat grains that will nourish your body and provide you with energy. Stay conscious of your chewing and swallowing. Relish the awareness you feel.

Once you've tried being more mindful, you'll begin to feel more peaceful and calm throughout the day. You can always practice mindfulness. Give it a try especially when you are wrapped up in what's coming next, instead of just what *is*.

The Escape Hatch

Everyone needs a mental trip once in a while. Have you ever been on a jog, on the bus, or in a sales meeting, and thought, "Come on, brain, think of something! Anything! Distract me from what's going on!" And it's weird, but you don't think of a thing. You may resort to trying to entertain yourself with melodramatic problems—"What about my mother-in-law? I usually can get going on that subject!"—to no avail; the event at hand dominates all attempts of mental escape.

One way to help solve this dilemma is to have a mental escape planned ahead of time. Take the time now to recreate a scene that you will remember later. Then, when you do need a mental escape hatch, you'll have one ready.

Naomi, a customer service representative, has a mental trip in place that she knows well, has spent time developing, and can imagine anywhere, anytime. She bases her locale on a trip she once took with her husband before they were married, and saw most everything through rose-colored lenses. Anytime she is stuck in an unfortunate situation, Naomi remembers her and her husband Eric's trip to Big Sur, California. She visualizes the winding road running along the coast, high above the crashing waves. The vast blue sky, the green tumultuous Pacific Ocean, and the jagged steep mountains—sheer beauty. She mentally arrives at her destination, a small wooded cabin, and can truly escape. The window looks out over the beach, where driftwood, rocks, and shells are scattered and waiting for an interested explorer.

Naomi remembers the smells of the ocean air and of the cypress trees, and the aroma of the firewood burning in their rented cabin. She remembers the textures, too—the soft throw rug on the old hardwood floors, and the firm but creaking bed with its heavy quilt. The trail down to the beach sounds crunchy as her bare feet walk over sand, dirt, and shells.

When she needs to, Naomi can picture and dream about her entire mental vacation scene, or she can choose to focus and expand on one aspect of it—like the fireplace, or the image of the ocean crashing onto the beach. You can do this as well. Spend one evening this week before you drift off to sleep putting an image together in your mind. Be sure to create one that you'll enjoy recalling whenever you're in a bind.

Letting Go of Stress

What good is a book on self-nourishment if it doesn't teach you how to let go of stress? To be a self-nurturer, you must possess a basic understanding of what causes stress, as well as be equipped with a couple of stress-freeing techniques.

Stress is not limited to negative events. In fact, according to the authors of *The Relaxation and Stress Reduction Workbook,* stress accompanies *any* change that must be adapted to—ranging from a negative extreme, such as acute physical danger, to the exhilaration of falling in love or achieving a long-desired success.

There are four basic sources that determine the impact of stress in your life: environment, social stressors, physiology, and thoughts. Your perception and interpretation of these situations determines whether they are "stressful" or "annoying," or "exciting" or "relaxing." If you were, say, an airline pilot, a trip in a Cessna airplane may simply be a relaxing, fun experience. If, however, you are a rather phobic flier, a trip in a Cessna may be interpreted differently—as a near-death experience, for instance.

Fortunately, there are ways to lighten your reactions to stress. First, be aware of your body's physiological reactions. Depending on how you personally deal with stress, you can learn ways to take care of it regularly. If you notice, for instance, that most of your tension is held in your head, you can learn relaxation and visualization exercises. If your body seems to hold a lot of your stress, try yoga or massage. For a quick start on reducing stress, the authors of *The Relaxation and Stress Reduction Workbook* suggest the following two techniques:

1. **The Tension Cutter**: First, take four abdominal breaths. Next, close your eyes and visualize your tension as either a color or a shape. It can be small or large, dark or light. Now imagine you are picking it up, turning it over in your hands and tossing it into the air as if it were a ball. Visualize your arm rearing back, in slow motion, preparing to throw the ball of tension. Now go ahead and pitch the ball of tension. Watch it disappear into the distance out of your awareness.

2. **Thought Substitution.** Perhaps you have a nagging thought that runs through your mind like a broken record. It is the source of some anxiety and probably is taking over your thoughts more than you realized. These kinds of thoughts can take on a life of their own. Try developing an alternative statement to tell yourself. For instance, you may tell yourself, "I'll never be able to solve that problem at work. There is no way this is going to turn out well!" Instead, tell yourself, even if you don't quite believe it at first, "I will do the very best that I can. I will resolve what is in my power to resolve, and this situation will pass. I will be okay." Your negative statement to yourself may begin to resolve, and, through the power of repetition, you may begin to see the truth in your alternative statement.

You may not have control over what life throws in your direction, but you do have some say as to how you respond to stressors. You have choices. Learn some basic stress-reducing techniques that work for you. These tools can help you to overcome most of the anxiety-filled challenges in your life.

Humor Heals

Remember the *Brady Brunch* episode when Marsha Brady had to take her driver's license test, and in order to relax she pictured her instructor in his underwear? Well, this is the working premise here—try to see the humor in tense or nerve-wracking situations, and you may come away feeling a little better.

The amusement is there, it's just a matter of stepping aside from your annoying circumstance long enough to note it. For instance, on your morning walk you may think, "Okay . . . this guy believes it's a big deal that I just yelled at his dog, which happens to be off his leash on my running trail and happens to be a pit bull with a chain link collar, but does the man have any idea that he looks like he could be his dog's biological father?" Sure, you could get caught up in the fact that you may have died in the jaws of an unleashed animal, but look on the funny side: Ha ha! The owner's mug is actually scarier than those jaws of death!

Kerryn Davis, a marketing researcher, relishes the opportunity for seeing normal or tense situations in different light. For instance, Kerryn remembers the first time she had dinner at her fiancé Gunter's parents' house. His parents enjoyed a pious existence: prim, proper, and, according to Kerryn, generally kind of frightening. Kerryn's upbringing in a liberal outlandish family straight out of the sixties did not lend itself well to such subdued situations. She started off the evening by accidentally explaining that her father was a "virgin" instead of a "surgeon," and that she was really enjoying her acupuncture treatments, "because there's nothing more relaxing than getting poked!" For the rest of the evening, Kerryn was so nervous that she chose to play the role of a mute rather than risk saying something else obscene.

The next time she went to Gunter's parents', she spent the hour beforehand having imaginary conversations with them in her mind, so she could just blurt out all of her secret fears, face them, laugh, and hopefully go on to have a nice evening. She imagined swearing every other word, "Can you please pass the damn asparagus, for fuck's sake?" Then Kerryn jumped around her apartment screeching and hollering to release her anxious energy. By the end of the hour, she was laughing, exhausted, and ready to take on the uptight atmosphere at her future in-laws house.

Next time you're in a tense situation, or even right afterward, try to identify some aspect of ridiculousness in the whole situation.

1. Associate the person with whom you are interacting in the face of your favorite comedian. For example, imagine your boss trying to intimidate Kramer from *Seinfeld* instead of your friend from work. What would Kramer have done that your friend didn't feel confident to do? Or Roseanne from *The Roseanne Show*. Would she have taken that kind of crap?

2. Imagine a comeback that you really wish you had said. For instance, if you were sitting on the subway and some jerk commented on your physique, imagine what you would've liked to have said to him as you were exiting the train: "Bye, Joe, and good luck with that deadbeat-dad legal charge."

3. Another good solution is to just pick up your favorite funny movies and spend the evening cracking up after a long day.

You can always choose to have yourself a good laugh and lighten up any tense moment. Laughing it off is good for you.

Stepping Out of Your Shell

Many people wish they could be more interactive and less inhibited in social situations. Perhaps your shyness is a budding pattern. Maybe you used to feel more socially adept, and just lately you haven't felt so outgoing. Or, maybe you've always been shy, but wouldn't mind experimenting with a few tried and true techniques that may help you to reach out more. It's not the easiest thing to just throw a small phobia or anxiety—such as shyness—out the window. Still, it's never too late to try stepping out, bit by bit.

Seth, a sweet, smart, and talented thirty-two-year-old, was always on the shy side; however, once his freelance writing career got going, he was isolated and even more bashful. His personality didn't change overnight, but he started to realize that because he had less and less exposure to people, his social skills were becoming a little creaky. It struck him once when a woman called for his roommate who wasn't home. Seth was in the middle of polishing up an article, absorbed in his thoughts, when she cracked some quick but small joke as they were hanging up. Seth was dead silent. He stuttered, said good-bye, and went back to working.

An hour later, Seth looked up and realized, "Shit! That joke was funny!" He laughed out loud at her comment, just a little too late. Then he realized, what the hell? When's the last time I just hung out and joked around, and felt *comfortable* doing so? He knew that he needed to start making an effort, just here and there, in small ways, so that he could become used to hearing his own voice, used to interacting, participating, and stirring his sense of humor back into action.

Seth made a pact to try something at least once a day—and you can, too. The three activities below will help you to step out of your shell. Even if you aren't immediately successful, or comfortable, you'll get used to interacting, and your skills won't be quite so petrified when you really need them.

1. **Speak to strangers**. It's time to break the first rule your parents taught you. You don't have to eat candy that strangers give you or get into a van that has no windows, just strike up small talk with people you don't know. In line at

the grocery store, or waiting for a bus, you can exchange simple pleasantries, such as "Nice weather, isn't it?" The more you interact, the more comfortable you'll become. Soon you might even be compelled to say something that truly is an expression of who you are, such as "You might want to avoid that carob-covered tofu you're buying, I tried it once and it's, uh, kinda weird . . ."

2. **Book club.** Discussing books provides an excellent venue for you to discover how you think about things. Additionally, it's an opportunity to hear how friends think differently about the very same issue. Sometimes, it can be better than group therapy. (According to Seth, cleaning the lint from the dryer is better than group therapy, but still . . .) You can join an already established book club or start one of your own. Seth started a book club with two friends, but eventually his friends brought their friends, and it grew to about seven people. They met once a month, and it became a wonderful way for everyone to get to know one another.

3. **Read the Sunday paper at a café.** In the old days, before steppin' out, Seth's only step out was to grab the paper off the porch in the morning. But the new Seth not only goes out to grab the paper, he keeps going—and you should, too. Off the porch, down the street, and straight to the local café to read the Sunday paper. Eventually, the people working and the other café patrons will get to know you and, after a while, may even greet you warmly when you come in for your Sunday latte.

With a little effort, you might start to enjoy exercising your social skills. It's like the old saying, "Use it or lose it!" If you're the shy type, start small, and don't pressure yourself to take the next step until you feel ready. Little by little, it'll become easier and be more fun.

Why Meditate?

The answer to why meditate could take volumes, or perhaps one simple, enlightening sentence. But a succinct response would need to be from the Dalai Lama, or another wise and eloquent yogi or monk.

There are many forms of meditation, ranging from strict and stationary to free-flowing movement. Suzie, an experienced yoga instructor, offers the following comments and tips on the art of meditation.

Whichever form of meditation you choose to do, the aim typically is to suspend extraneous thoughts and to somehow reconnect with something deeper within, deeper than your daily worries, anxieties, fears, anger, or fatigue.

Try the following meditative exercise: Close your eyes and imagine for a moment a candle flame. Try to empty your mind of all else besides this flame. How long does it take before thoughts enter? Do you begin to think of deadlines, your children's schoolwork, your upcoming cocktail party, and so on? These are all thought invaders that keep you from experiencing the *now*, or your inner, deeper self. Picture the flame again. Every time your mind begins to wander, let it go, notice thoughts entering into your mind, and then go back to the flame. You may go back to imagining the flame twenty times. This is okay. It's the mind's natural tendency to think, so don't be hard on yourself.

If you try meditating for five minutes a day for a few weeks, you'll start to notice how meditation can work for you. As you repeatedly focus your mind on your flame, or perhaps a mantra (such as repeating the word "Om"), you are learning to *focus inward*. In their book *The Daily Relaxer*, Matt McKay and Pat Fanning point out the following benefits of meditation:

- It is extremely difficult to worry, fear, or hate because your mind is focusing on something other than these emotions.

- It isn't necessary to think about everything that pops into your head. You have the ability to choose which thoughts you think.

- Aside from the thoughts and pictures in your mind, emotion consists of entirely physical sensations in your body. Even the strongest emotions will become manageable if you concentrate on the sensations in your body, and not the content of the thought that produced the emotion.

- Thought and emotion are not permanent. They pass into and out of your body and mind. They need not leave a trace.

When you are aware of what is happening in the here and now, the extreme highs and lows of your emotional response to life will disappear. You will live life with equanimity.

There are endless reasons and ways you can enjoy meditation, but if this is a new endeavor, start simple and see what comes up for you.

Taking a Mitty Break

A half century ago, James Thurber wrote a classic story called, "The Secret Life of Walter Mitty." In the tale, Mitty leads a meek and uneventful life. He's a "yes dear" sort of guy. But in his imagination dwells an altogether different man. Mitty is an indomitable pilot saving his crew during a hurricane; he's a great surgeon called in for only the most difficult cases; he's a brilliant witness who confounds and then punches out the district attorney.

While his wife dithers about whether he bought biscuits for the dog, Mitty laughs in the face of oblivion. He's preparing to run an impossible gauntlet on his lone mission to destroy enemy forces. His face is set in a small, ironic smile as cannons and mortars pound the no-man's-land beyond the trenches—drowning out the car and traffic and his wife's suggestion that he really should wear gloves this time of year.

Something in this story touches a chord. Partly it's how we all struggle not to drown in the commonplace and ordinary. But mostly it's that heroic fantasies are a secret pleasure in which many of us, at one time or another, have indulged. Think back. Wasn't there a prize you once visualized yourself winning? Haven't you imagined doing or saying something that friends would admire? Have you ever imagined yourself saving or standing up for someone? Have you ever pictured yourself vanquishing the bad guy, or saying the most incredibly healing and comforting thing to someone in pain?

Over the years, you may have enjoyed a number of Mittyesque fantasies, seeing yourself accomplished, triumphant, heroic. It feels good. You are, for a few moments, the person you always wanted to be. These fantasies actually send a message to your unconscious that you are *capable* of doing some of the things that you admire. The very act of visualizing an ideal self makes it more possible. Or even likely.

Heroic and accomplishment fantasies are a genuine form of self-nourishment. They can help you escape a dull or stressful present. They can give you hope—not so much that you'll achieve *le grande triomphe*, but that you can be and do things closer to your ideal self. If not a hero, at least someone capable. Someone well thought of. They can also motivate you to try things, take risks, reach for the brass ring.

A Mitty break doesn't take long—it can certainly be less than five minutes. Just fire up your imagination and visualize:

- some form of recognition for work you do or want to do
- a situation that forces you to show your best stuff
- a moment where you display strength and style
- an achievement, a mission accomplished
- a crisis that you overcome
- a moment of caring and generosity

The ideal times for Mitty breaks are while commuting, while listening to your sister-in-law blather on the phone, during boring sermons or lectures, during coffee breaks, while grocery shopping, while pretending to read the newspaper, in the bath tub, doing gardening. In short, while engaged in anything that doesn't require your full attention. You might even try it right now . . .

Part V

Sexy Time-Outs

We are, as a culture, unequivocally obsessed with sex. Sexual images and messages and services run so rampant that it's astonishing people ever accomplish anything besides copulation. Yet most of us actually have sex for relatively few minutes each week. You don't have to be told something is askew with that ratio; but is it possible that the problem lies in the ways people think (or don't think) about sex?

Sexuality, the way it's normally packaged, is not so much about satisfaction as it is about conquest. Most of the magazine-and-TV-style rhetoric about sex is terribly disempowering to the media-hungry public. It teaches that you're never good enough and that there is always something to fix: Are you thin enough to have good sex? Are you having the right kind of sex? Are you having enough sex? Too much sex? The questions beckon and rob your soul of its own natural approach to sexuality and sensuality.

Gratefully, there is much more to sexuality than just the physical act of having sex. And though it's certainly true that having a good sex life can be wonderful for mental health, it's equally enriching to spend time mulling sex over, rolling it around in your mind. It is fun to take a break for a few moments from the over-sexualized world we live in and simply *think* about sex—or sexiness.

This section provides a variety of sexy time-out suggestions. A sexy time-out can be a fleeting fantasy, or an intentional flight from the norm of your sex life. It can be shared or solo. In short, a sexy time-out can be anything you want it to be—but the trick is you have to think about it. (Think about sex? That doesn't sound too difficult.)

You will see how important a secret, unconsummated crush can be to wellness. You'll find out how the simple act of wearing something special under your work clothes can provide delicious private amusement. You'll see how sexy it can be to rethink sex. You'll discover what it is that you think is sexy. The following pages provide suggestions on how to take your sexuality back into your own hands . . . instead of depleting, let it restore.

Feeling Sexy

What makes someone sexy? In many ways, it's about how you express your-self—how your inner strength comes through in your everyday activities, the way you express your intellect, your artistic nature, your physical abilities, the way your passion shines in your eyes when you talk excitedly about something you want to accomplish—these can all be sexy characteristics, qualities that make you feel sexy, and are sexy to others, too.

Think about it, who do you think is sexy? Imagine someone in your life—your partner, someone you work with or go to school with, someone in your carpool, etc. Once you have someone in mind, think about what makes that person sexy to you. Most likely, it isn't the standard formula beauty, but it's the person's particular little nuances that make them irresistibly sexy—the way she places one hand on her hip and looks so severe when she gives directions, or the way he slightly tilts his head as he grins down at you, or the way she crosses her legs so that one long slender leg shows off a delicate ankle contour.

Sex appeal is not simply a set of perfectly straight Farrah Fawcett teeth or an obviously over-aerobicized butt. When Sarah, a thirty-five-year-old book editor, was in college, she was instantly attracted to the quiet boys, the ones who set up camp under a tree and read large unwieldy books—soooo sexy. These boys *must* be having deep thoughts . . . (of course, as she came to find out, sometimes these boys were sim-ply have shallow meaningless thoughts, no matter how shy and introspective they appeared).

Just as others have this appeal, so do you have slight and subtle quirks that express who you are—and these qualities are sexy. Your sense of humor, your talents, the way you emphasize an opinion with a gesture, you are probably loaded with beautiful, noticeable nuances that you aren't aware of or have forgotten. Take a look. Think about it. What makes you feel sexy? Take stock of who you are and how you express this, and have fun with your sexiness. Do you enjoy the way it feels when you go on a hike and feel strong and physical? When you feel your body move, when each stride flexes your leg muscles? Or maybe you feel sexy when you smell beautiful, or wear something soft or silky.

Start tomorrow morning on a sexy note:

1. Even if no one else notices, even if no one else will see, wear something sexy under you normal, everyday clothes. Buy some new underwear—whatever feels sexy to you—they make sexy underwear for men and women. Sarah loves sexy gender-bending undergarments, a thin Marlon Brando-style men's sleeveless tank top–under her work blouse, with black panties. This has a tough and a sexy feel—strong, but feminine. Or, go out and buy a pair of panties you never thought you'd wear, bright red lace or a deep purple velvet underwear set. If you're a guy, you have options, too (maybe the ones already mentioned!). Calvin Klein makes sexy boy briefs, and there are many generic take-offs. Whatever your taste, pick out some tantalizing undies and don them on just a regular old working day.

2. Before starting your day, take a bath with essential oils. Add some lavender, rose, or a musky-scented oil, and all day you'll have sensual smelling skin. Or just use a scented body lotion, and spread it thoroughly over your skin. Vanilla, gardenia, or sandalwood scents will provide a clean and scrumptious appeal.

The Secret Crush

You make yourself available to their schedule, on the off chance of bumping into them. You hang on their every word, infusing their thoughts with meaning only you could understand. They're your soul mate, your perfect lover, your dream spouse . . . only you're never, ever going to let them know about your feelings. That's the charm of them. They're yours in secret, and they haven't, nor will they ever have, any idea.

Have you ever had a secret crush on a coworker? On your partner's best friend? On your own best friend? You wouldn't dream of upsetting the larger picture of the relationship by exposing your "true" feelings. And that's not even the point. Crushes fade. They don't last. Sometimes they turn into real love, which you do have to attend to and do something about; but more times than not, crushes float away, returning you to that blessed state of platonic affection. What crushes do is put you in touch with your perfect projected self, and also with your (sometimes hidden) emotional goals. Besides being tantalizing, crushes can be very useful emotional tools.

Have you ever had a crush sneak right up on you? You're going along, in a friendship or an acquaintanceship or whatever, and something changes overnight: a nuanced glance, a gesture, and suddenly you're hooked. (Recall the episode of *Seinfeld* when George Costanza had a sudden and ridiculous attraction to Elaine Benes, one of his closest friends, after he heard her whispering a voice message.) But just as soon as a crush comes on, it's probably going to pass. What's happening is you're responding to something you think you're being offered, and whether you are or aren't, that's a good time to look at what your need is telling you.

What does a crush reveal? It's not just about your gonads, to be sure. First of all, it says that there is hope in your world. To be crushed out, even secretly, is to have a certain sheen of hope on your worldview. Secondly, it tells you about what you value. If you're interested in your mechanic, look closer at his or her features: Is she honest and hardworking? Is he prompt, or really funny? Thirdly, it speaks to your essence. Who you are informs who you want your ideal partner to be. If you're attracted to bird lovers, chances are you love birds yourself, or at least a part of you does.

It's important to recognize and validate how having a crush is serving your needs. Pay close attention to how you feel around the person on whom you have a crush. Do you feel expansive, like you could do anything or be anyone? Smart? Attractive? Do you admire the qualities they possess? Do you wish you could be more like them or have the kind of life they have? If you feel really good around the person, it could be that they mirror your ideal self, that is, the self you want to be. The beauty of secret crushes is that you can learn so much about yourself. Because having a crush is usually a solo act, and not a relationship you have to be accountable to, you can use your findings for personal enrichment.

Much is made of crushes, and there's commonly a lot of societal shaming about them. We say, use them. Divine your truest thoughts through the lens of a crush. Dive deep into it, while at the same time keeping your head above water. Because they're fleeting, learn what you can while you can.

The Spice of Good Fantasies

Reality, to say the least, has its limitations. Nowhere is this more true than in our sexual lives. Our desires keep colliding with romantic bogeymen that show up in the form of headaches, tiredness, irritation, fear of embarrassment, or fear of rejection.

Because reality is so often less than we'd like it to be, why not spice up life's dull moments with a well-made sexual fantasy? It's a good way to enjoy yourself while commuting, waiting, working out, or getting ready to fall asleep. You can craft scenes that are full of sweet, hesitating steps of early romance, or full-tilt athletic events. You can create experiences that are fun to imagine, but too dangerous or embarrassing to actually do. You can revisit old lovers, or make it with movie stars. You can be aggressive, or be taken care of in ways no real lover has ever accomplished.

Fantasy can be more than a pleasant break on a dull day. It's also a way to rehearse and become comfortable with new experiences. Sexual fantasies sometimes prepare us for trying new things in real life. Or they allow us to imagine the kind of relationship and kind of partner that could best meet our sexual and emotional needs. So our fantasies can become a guide, showing us what we really want and providing the motivation to look for it.

Nancy Friday, Lonnie Garfield Barbach, and other writers have been encouraging women for years to enrich and explore their sexual fantasies. And they give several good reasons. The first is simple: Fantasies feel good. Second, fantasies increase sexual awareness and sexual interest. They also allow us to experience, without fear of judgment, a fuller range of situations that are arousing. And finally, fantasies are great distractions from a lot of life's bummers.

Here are some suggestions to maximize fantasy enjoyment:

- Create some fantasies that are long, even complex, scenarios. Then you can dip in and out, starting and stopping the scene like a videotape.

- Try to include imagery from what you see, hear, and feel in each fantasy. Using all three of these sense modalities makes the experience feel more real.

- Give each fantasy an emotional richness by focusing on texture, temperature, lighting, smell, the murmur of conversation—anything that evokes a sense of mood.

- Let the scene build—don't start right at the big moment. Create some sexy dialogue, some delicious lead-up, and foreplay.

- Enjoy variations on a theme. If there's something exciting about a particular scene, try imagining it with little additions and embroideries on the plot. Change the dialogue. Substitute new "actors."

- Develop a few brief fantasies that are good while you're waiting at a fast-food drive-through, or during a commercial on TV.

- Try new things, perhaps what you'd be too embarrassed to explore with a partner. Or exciting things you'd never really want to happen. It's okay. Nothing can hurt you in your imagination.

Napoleon once said, "Imagination rules the world." But more accurately, it makes its own world. And that's what you're encouraged to do—create a world for your own pleasure and enjoyment. A place that's all about what feels good to you. A stage where every actor, every prop, every gesture, and every line exists solely to make an empty moment more exciting.

Location, Location, Location

The inimitable game show host, Bob Eubanks, would routinely inquire of his guests on *The Newlywed Game*, "Where's the craziest place you two ever made whoopee?" The blushing beehive bride would look to her bemused groom, who would look back at her, and tentatively hold up a cue card with "Attic at Grandma's House" written on it. Then the shy bride would turn into an eye-rolling warrior, bashing her new husband with a cue card that says, "Cemetery." It's been proven: Variety is the spice of life. Upsetting your regular sexual routine by trying a new location can really shake things up, in a good way.

Increased adrenaline can lead to heightened senses. We're not suggesting that you grab a sexual partner and run naked to Times Square for some live nudie street action. The idea here is that it can be incredibly erotic and fun to mix things up a bit in the area of sexual sites. Regress, if you will, to the days of trying with your girlfriend to get to as many bases as you could with your brother just in the next room . . . that was sexy! You could be caught at any time. The thrill of the unlocked door, the knickers off, and the music blasting . . . it was intoxicating.

Well, you can have that kind of thrill (or a version of it) again. You don't have to totally get down to business to steal a sexy new location moment. If the spirit moves you, plant an unexpected and smoldering kiss on your husband while you're waiting for a table in a restaurant. Slip an erotic note into your lover's pocket while you're watching a movie. Remind her about it on the way home. Suggest that you pull over, just for a minute. There is no rule that grown people, even long-term lovers, cannot make out in cars.

For the more location-adventurous, you probably don't need advice, but here's hoping the more timid will learn and explore: If you can find a drive-in movie theater anywhere, go to see any movie playing (do not discriminate) and have yourself a jolly, sexy time. There's something about public privacy that lends itself well to erotic adventurousness. Look into private outdoor hot tubs, especially when it's raining. And do go to the cemetery. It might not be all that respectful of the deceased, but it can be pretty sexy fun.

Part VI

Checking In with Yourself

The following pages pay homage to the Self—dignified, integrated, and grounded. By now you're familiar with the notion of self-nourishment in its many forms. For the next and final chapter, the nourishing focus is on the depth of the human experience, the stuff on which philosophy is founded.

The following pages will encourage you to get in touch with your creative yearnings to recognize your essential self in a complicated world. They will ask you to get private. They will ask you to get simple. They will ask you to think seriously and deeply about your purpose in life.

Whether you're learning more about subjects in which you've always been interested, or you're creating quiet time exclusively for personal exploration, the following exercises will remind you that there may still be a lot of parts of yourself that you haven't even met. Lucky you.

Hey, Where Did I Go?

Similar to the way you can misplace your keys, your wallet, your most important tax forms, and the like, you can also misplace yourself. Not your physical body, obviously, but all of those special little quirks that used to remind you of who and why you were the way you were. You know, you may be the only one who really ever appreciated the perfectly breaded corn dog. Rachel, an elementary school teacher, remembers clearly being the only one in her family who'd take immense pleasure from the 1970s gold-specked mirror that ran the length of her entrance staircase. She liked the way it distorted her image. As she walked up the stairs she'd try to create a new distortion—sometimes it was Rachel's nose that would dominate her reflection, other times it was her left eye, and so on.

It's both fun and positive to revisit the idiosyncrasies from your past that remind you of your unique perspectives on life, the stuff not many people know about you. The clues are everywhere, in old journals, your favorite novel from high school or college, photos hidden in shoeboxes, music tapes, etc. While it's true that such items should perhaps remain out of sight for everyone's sake, there is a time and a place for everything—and now is one of those times. Spend one hour, while no one else is in your house, and dig a few of these goodies up. Start with just two—an old journal and a favored novel from the past.

- **Old Journals**: With such memorable lines as "I had that recurring dream again . . . what does it mean?? The one where I am traveling through the land of English-muffin people wearing fleece vests. . . ," rereading journal entries can make you chuckle. But old journals can serve a more important purpose than just humor: They are the landmarks of your life, the path you have walked to bring you to wherever you are now. Notice old insights or first impressions—maybe you're not as silly as you thought you were. Maybe you'll even recognize the beginnings of certain personal growth patterns. When you see this, give yourself a pat on the back. It's easy to criticize and judge yourself without even realizing it. But stop, look how far you've come!

- **Favorite novels**: What was one of your most cherished novels in the past? If you're a book lover, you probably have moved from one apartment to another lugging boxes of books, every time wondering, why in the hell do I hold on to these?! You know why? Because they were all small love affairs—small, bound pages that you poured over for a whole weekend, summer, or winter. So just what was it about those heroines or heroes you loved so much? Was it their adventurous spirit, wit, charm? Why did these characters mean so much to you? The answers to these questions can often point to characteristics within you that make up who you are—your likes, dislikes, your preference for, say, the sweet loner in a story as opposed to admiration for the money-hungry landowner.
- For Rachel, it was Franny from J. D. Salinger's *Franny and Zooey*. All Rachel has to do is pick up this thin paperback and she's instantly transported. Franny, the character who took all of her ideals so seriously, as if they were all that mattered in life, now there was a heroine! Franny wasn't concerned with getting to the commuter bus on time, or worried about her phone bill—no, Franny was concerned about life, purpose, phonies, and saints. Franny captivated Rachel's romantic soul, as she still can. That's why Rachel keeps her around—who else besides Franny can bring up those qualities so immediately?

Who or what brings up your treasured ideals and idiosyncrasies? Hold on to that novel, those old journals, no matter how many times you move. And remember to revisit them every now and again. They're all a part of who you are and where you come from. (That's what you can tell the movers or your friends who have to lug those boxes up three flights during your next move . . .).

Nourishment for Mom or Dad

"He took my elephant!"

"I don't *wanna* wear my rain boots! I didn't make it rain!"

"I want a coooookie! Now!"

Most parents love their children more than life itself. Even the most stoic of new parents will confess that they'd never felt anything so strong as the kind of love between them and their child(ren). Children are engaged in an incredible developmental battle from the time they're born until they leave the house (and forever after). As a parent, you can empathize with your child's struggle to learn everything there is to know about life at a light-speed pace. But sometimes, enough's enough!

As a parent, you need to take care of yourself, as the cliché goes, or else you're no good to anybody. From the overwhelm parents experience during the infant months, to the power-struggling toddler years, and beyond, parents are focused with such intensity on their children that they themselves sometimes disappear. They commonly sabotage their individual lives by falling into the "I have to be the perfect mother or father" trap at the expense of taking some personal time to be themselves.

This was especially true for Maura, a thirty-three-year-old mother of a baby girl. A scientist, Maura was very invested in controlling her environment. She didn't like surprises or unpredictability. Maura spent the first nearly four months of her daughter's life trying to predict and control everything—a disappointing prospect. Like most new parents, Maura was uncomfortable letting anyone else take care of her baby, not even so she could peacefully eat a meal. She wouldn't let her husband comfort the baby at night either, assuming only she could give her daughter the best care. Exhausted, hungry, and short-tempered, this did not at all fit into Maura's vision of angelic, perfect motherhood.

Frustrated, Maura decided to try to let go of a lot of the control she thought she needed at home. She began very slowly, first by asking her husband to comfort the baby during the night. After a week, feeling more rested, she decided to finally take some time for herself. First just an hour in the afternoon, then two, then dinner out, then dinner and a movie. It was very difficult at first to refrain from calling the baby-sitter every two minutes to check on things at home. But pretty soon she could really relax, and she allowed herself to actually look forward to her time away from the family.

These days, Maura is a pro at taking care of herself. She has nurtured many extra-household pursuits, such as joining a moonlight hiking group and taking a furniture-making class. She knows that without attending to herself, she risks disappearing altogether. Her family life is all the richer for it.

It's important to make time for yourself, especially when you're a parent. Every month, try to commit to doing at least two of the following activities alone:

- Sign-up for a class
- Go to therapy
- Take a walk or a run
- Read in a café
- Spend time with friends
- Attend a movie

Take care of yourself. Your children will thank you, eventually.

Dealing with Life's Major Transitions

You've moved out of state . . . You're in the middle of a divorce. . . You've broken your leg . . . You got a new job . . . You've fallen in love . . . Major transitions are big deals. Whether the catalyst for change is good or bad, transitions almost always lead to stress.

Peter can attest to the stress-transition factor that accompanies big changes. He was married in the spring, and in the winter his wife took a job out of state. Peter lived in the same state all his life and was deeply rooted. Beyond the fact that moving meant he would have to find another job, as well as have to face a host of other changes, he was totally defiant about leaving the safety and security of his home-town. He knew he should be treating the move as an adventure, but instead he felt terribly resistant to and irritated by the whole situation. Because of his reluctance, Peter's wife, starved for his support, was not at all excited about the prospect of start-ing her new career.

After they moved, it took Peter and his wife a full year to finally feel "right" in their new surroundings. The stress almost caused them to break up. Once things calmed down, however, and they could look around at the life they'd created together, they began to feel proud of themselves, and the spirit of adventure was able to seep into their daily lives.

Change changes you, no matter what. It's something to survive, even if the new force is positive. Think about falling in love. It's a sweeping, life-altering phenome-non that takes a long time to process, even when the relationship is good and sup-portive. Transitions are like that, too. Because they're unavoidable, it's important to have the internal resources to cope with them. Perhaps you're embroiled in a big transitional phase of life right now, or maybe you have recently experienced a big shift. How did you cope?

The following basic strategies will help you to gear up for life's upcoming, inev-itable transitions.

- **Stay flexible**. Rigidity can be responsible for a number of coping-saboteurs: isolation, resentment, low self-esteem, and stress. Consider your muscles: If you try to lift something too heavy without warming up and stretching, you are at risk for injury. Likewise, if you try to cling to the familiar, dismissing anything new while change is all around you, you risk hurting yourself.

- **Be curious**. Curiosity equals hope. Hope buoys.

- **Remain centered**. Know that you are who you are no matter what you must deal with; honor yourself.

- **Reach out for help when you need it**. It does no one any good if you're suffering and not asking for help.

- **Remember that transition always leads to growth**. Though it may not seem so at the time, you'll eventually reap the rich rewards of having gotten through a big transition, and knowing yourself all the better for it.

Perhaps the most nourishing commitment you can make to yourself is to prioritize your mental and physical health every day, especially when you're dealing with big changes or are in the midst of major transitions.

Professor Me– Personal Learning Projects

What do Fidel Castro and Francis Ford Coppola have in common? Well, on the face of it, maybe not much. But if you're engaged in a Professor Me personal learning project, you might find that they can be linked in a number of interesting ways.

Many of us yearn for our college days when our focus purely was on learning. True enough, most of us don't miss the deadlines and the papers, but immersing ourselves in subjects about which we were passionate—that was fun.

You can reclaim that feeling for yourself very simply . . . host your own survey course—a personal learning project—on a topic in which you are interested. You can do this as a solo project or as a group effort. It involves two elements: curiosity and a bit of research. The result is the satisfaction of an intellectual hunger that all of us have, but perhaps have lost touch with.

What makes your pulse quicken, even for a second? Is it the thought of you traveling to distant shores? Learning more about fine art? Discovering the nuances of famous detective stories? Once you've identified what it is that you're hankering for, the next step is to acquire more information about it. This is your opportunity to become an expert. The theme could resonate with the ordinary , or it could be a total departure from it. For research, you can use movies, videos, books, music, the Internet, and more. From how many different angles can you examine a subject? Consider history, geography, sports and leisure, entertainment, literature, and science. Each new area will lead to a new thought or a new chunk of information.

You can use the Professor Me series to explore subjects about which you've often wondered, but might not know much, such as film noir. Or you can use it as a powerful teaching tool. For example, although you've read bits and pieces about the Vietnam War, you still may not understand exactly what happened or when. If you choose one good history book to read, a few movies to view (documentaries and dramatic, big-budget films, like *Platoon*)—and a few weeks later you're more of an expert.

Or maybe you and your friends all share an interest in the music of the Beatles. You could have a Beatles book group for a few months, read all the biographical accounts of their careers, and then get together and talk about it once a week, listening to and talking about their music in a more informed way. You can turn the gathering into a drinking game, or a cunning game of prediction, complete with prizes/services awarded for correct guesses. Not only is it intellectually stimulating, but it can also be an elixir for the heart.

Some tips for your Professor Me series:

- **Designate, on average, about six weeks for your course**.
- **Make it a group pursuit**. Additional people lend a variety of sensibility and expertise. You and three friends can meet once a week to present various pieces of the puzzle. It could be a Saturday morning breakfast or a Thursday-after-work gathering. Groups are great for working on a topic when each participant knows different aspects about the same subject.

Keep your Professor Me personal learning project fun. Remember that the point of the course isn't to bore you, it's to advance you a bit further along on the human enrichment continuum.

Private Time

There's a story, probably apocryphal, that Greta Garbo used to don some carefully selected rags and go out publicly as a bag lady. She'd do anything to maintain her privacy. One of the Marx Brothers reportedly answered his own door disguised as the butler. On these occasions, needless to say, he was never "in."

Hiding out isn't just for celebrities. A friend of Matt's used to answer the phone in a thick Irish brogue, telling the caller she was the cleaning lady and alone in the house. "Shall I leave a note, dear? Or do you want to wait a wee bit and call back? My, but this phone is dusty." Another friend had a sign he'd put up on his office door that read, "Pretending I'm Not Here." Matt, himself, used to stop a little-used freight elevator between floors at work. No one could see or bother him, and he'd happily read there for twenty minutes undisturbed.

The point here is that we all need private time. A few minutes when we can relax, and not have to respond to anyone. When we can let our minds drift, and let the world go completely. Human beings are wired to need periods when their circuits go down. We need to withdraw. If we stay always "on," always in contact, we literally burn out with exhaustion. If we try to stop the natural oscillation between contact, coping, involvement, and withdrawal we fall prey to a myriad of stress-related illnesses.

A very big key to emotional balance and physical well-being is to have private time each day—both scheduled and found. To schedule private time, literally write it in your appointment book. Some of the best times are during lunch, between appointments, a break while you're driving somewhere, right after work, or following dinner. Be sure to set it in your mind—and schedule it—at the beginning of each day so you can plan for these periods of hiding out.

For some people, it helps to schedule private time at exactly the same hour and location each day. The routine will reinforce your commitment to allow yourself this space. But planning isn't everything. Look for *opportunities* to withdraw, found moments when you can let go for a few minutes. Ideally, these should include:

- a closed door so people aren't watching you trying to relax. Or worse, aren't tempted to interrupt you
- physical comfort
- a sense that you have at least ten or twenty minutes where you don't have to do anything
- reasonable quiet
- an attitude of passivity, letting your mind go where it wants to. No trying to fix or solve anything
- a willingness to stop intrusion—not answering the phone or door, or asking people to wait

Private time can be a big source of nourishment. It can make a hard day bearable; it can make a good day splendid. Remember, it's not healthy for you to be "on" all the time. Hiding out heals and replenishes.

Creative Journaling

Of Human Bondage author W. Somerset Maugham drew the scenes and characters of his novels from a vast collection of notes and observations that he started keeping as a teenager. When he finally published *A Writer's Notebook*, at the age of seventy, it was excerpted from a journal of thousands of pages that he had been writing for more than fifty years.

It was in this storehouse of experience that Maugham recorded the quality of light in an Alpine town, the texture of a sandstone cliff face, as well as the quirks and traits, gestures and expressions of hundreds of people he encountered.

The great poet, Rainer Maria Rilke, had an entirely different theory about writing. He advised looking inward rather than outward, exploring memory and textures of feeling rather than talking about the outer world. "Think of the world you carry within you," he said. "Remember your own childhood and yearnings. Be attentive to what rises up in you, and set it above everything that you observe around you."

Whether you are like Maugham or Rilke, whether you focus on sensory or on inner experience, creative journaling is a way to deepen your appreciation of life. It's nourishing to spend a little time each day reflecting on the images, experiences, and feelings that stand out; noticing what seems most meaningful. Then finding words to describe what you saw and heard and felt.

Creative journaling is a chance to experience a deeper sense of yourself. It quiets, momentarily, the headlong rush through life so you can be the observer as well as the actor in the play. So you can linger awhile over a scene, seeing again the quality of light, hearing once more some piece of dialogue.

Creative journaling is different from keeping a diary. Both diary and journal are made from words, but a diary records, whereas writing in a journal evokes. Journaling recreates the experience; it brings it to life on the page. If you'd like to explore creative journaling, the following guidelines may be helpful:

- Spend time journaling each day. Try to journal at the same point in the day—following a particular meal, or just after you crawl into bed.

- In the beginning, try the discipline of focusing on only a single moment in the day. Choose the moment intuitively, without thought. You don't have to know what that moment or image means, just that it means something.

- Let your journal writing surprise you. Write without knowing where you're going, without any preconception of what you want to say.

- Start with a concrete description, but choose things to describe that *suggest* your emotion. In fact, let a shadow or texture or movement *be* the emotion.

- After each description, add the "connectives." These are memories, images, feelings, or thoughts that somehow connect to the moment you described. You don't have to understand how they're related, just write them down and notice your reactions.

Right now, get your pen and a spiral notebook. This is a good time to start. What's the one thing that happened today that seems the most worth writing about. . . .

Simplicity

Get on that treadmill—and go, go, go, go, go! Get shopping! Get to buying! Think you have enough? Think again! There's always something else—until you're covered in catalogs and price tags and wrapping and debt. It's not your fault—blame the media. Blame your parents for not giving you enough love. Blame the credit card companies who descend on you in college and offer you "money" you wouldn't ordinarily have. Blame away, but that won't solve the problem of the hunger that consumerism creates. Rather than being nourishing, relentless chasing after "the thing" that will assuage life's woes is downright depleting.

This week, engage in an exercise that will challenge the consumer industry: Spend seven days being fully conscious of every cent you spend. While that might not seem relaxing, you will feel rewarded by week's end. Its nourishing properties are many:

- **Less spending equals more savings**. Maybe this is obvious, but sometimes we ignore this basic truth. When we spend less, we have more. It's simple. And more is better, right?

- **Control over impulses**. Reflect on what it feels like to "need" some material thing . . . a tingling in the abdomen, a yearning pull in the chest, sometimes nausea. Not coincidentally, those feelings are also the hallmarks of addiction. Imagine that every time you feel desperately drawn to new finials for the curtains or whatever, a destructive force is beckoning you. It's time to squelch that slavish instinct to buy, and realize that no one absolutely *needs* new finials. It feels right to not be in the acquisitions race, even for just a week.

- **Strengthen creative thinking**. Being proactive about fun requires more energy than going to a movie. It's more interesting and fulfilling to get out of the passive, "Here's my money . . . entertain me!" mode. Sit down and think about how you'd like to amuse yourself. If you naturally think of expensive ways to get your jollies, try to translate them into the same idea, only more homespun (and therefore, simpler). For example, perhaps you like the the-

122

ater, but those tickets cost an arm and a leg. So go to the library and check out the written form of your favorite play. Either read it solo or invite friends over to have a reading.

In addition to tracking every penny you spend, here are additional ideas that will help you keep it simple this week:

- **Use your brain**. Be inventive with how you use your free time. Don't use a lack of lavish spending as an excuse to become bored.

- **Make something out of nothing**. By creating something from scratch, you'll end up with a lasting and useful object and the satisfaction of having created it yourself.

- **Forget your credit card**. Every day, take with you only exactly the amount of cash you want to spend. Try not to spend an extra cent if you can help it. Of course, if you have to commute or you have regular, anticipated expenses, set those aside. But if you tend to spend money on lunch, coffee, and extravagances, then think again. When bills come, pay them by the next day. Don't let anything pile up. Stay on top of it.

Instead of going for the quick fix, the empty and falsely satiating instant gratification, stop and *think*. What are you *really* yearning for? Some creativity? Some intellectual stimulation? Don't let your society fool you—you can take care of such needs without consuming or going into debt. Think simply; think simplicity.

On Purpose

West Coast surfer, Diana, spent five years freezing her extremities off in a graduate program in the Midwest. She had waffled forever about the wisdom of entering into a long and intense program, but she ultimately acquiesced to her practical side (with familial urgings), bit the bullet, and set out to become a psychologist. For most of her half decade of immersion, she was despondent; her hair started falling out, she was having regular panic attacks ... at times, she was barely hanging on.

Diana would sometimes reach out to her friends back home and whisper into the phone, almost afraid of her own thoughts, "I don't think I even like psychology. I wish I could just be a bartender. Seriously." This would not shock her friends, who always knew Diana as a social butterfly/life-of-the-party. Originally she set out to earn a degree in an area she knew she was good at: counseling. Turns out, though, being good at something doesn't necessarily equal loving it, or even liking it. And, apparently, sometimes it'll even make your hair fall out.

Identifying and pursuing your passion takes real courage, but the rewards are obvious and plentiful. Understanding and nurturing your purpose can affect your psychological state, energy, and stress levels in profound ways. The first step to living your purpose is to identify and acknowledge your deepest hopes for yourself, the ones that you might have shoved way back in the closet by the uncomfortable shoes. Here's an exercise to get you thinking about your purpose, from which you can extrapolate your passion.

Imagine you only have six months to live. Would you want to change anything in your life? How drastically? Next, imagine you have unlimited resources. You can do whatever you want, because money is not an issue. What would you do? Lastly, imagine a typical day in your ideal occupation and lifestyle. Mentally describe the entire day in detail, from waking up, to working, to evening activities. Pay close attention to your home and work environment. What are your tasks? Who are the people surrounding you in your ideal day? Complete this exercise by mentally sailing through various periods in your life—fifteen to twenty-five years old, twenty-five to thirty-five years old, and beyond—when during those years did you feel truly absorbed?

Now, open your eyes, get out a piece of paper or your journal, and make a list of the following:

- Activities you'd like to try
- Strengths and accomplishments in all of life's components
- Qualities and achievements for which you'd most like to be remembered
- Characteristics you remember most in others

Don't let your mind curtail your dreams based on any perceived limitations: physical, financial, social, etc. List all the things you want to do, be, share, and have. Keep writing for at least fifteen minutes. Describe people, feelings, and places. Review and identify major themes. Then, write a paragraph, summarizing your themes and thinking of ways to make them a concrete aspect of your life. Clarify the saliency of your themes by talking with your partner or a good friend, someone who always has the "best you" in mind.

Grounding

You've heard the expressions, "His feet are on the ground," or "She's really down to earth." These are usually compliments for someone who is realistic, clear, and honest. It seems to follow that the more aware we are of our connection to the earth—that is, *being grounded*—the more comfortable we feel in our bodies and our lives.

Noticing where our bodies intersect with the world—what presses on our feet, butt, back, and elbows—is the first step to feeling clear about who we are and what we're doing. It's like having basic coordinates on our place in the universe.

Grounding is always about what's happening *right now*. Where our body is *now*; what it feels like *now*; what's happening emotionally *now*. And because grounding forces us to be in the present, to experience ourselves at this exact moment, it makes us honest with ourselves. It provides us something very real to stand on when dealing with the outer world—the solid ground of our true feelings.

If all this sounds like new-age hokum, forget it. Just do the grounding exercise. You'll like it. It will help you feel strong and refreshed. If the *concept* of grounding makes intuitive sense to you, then experience the exercise as a window through which you can know yourself more clearly. Here's what to do:

- Close your eyes and place your feet flat on the floor. Feel the pressure of the floor against your soles. Pay attention to whether the sensation is pleasant or unpleasant.

- Now notice your other points of contact with the world. Feel the pressure of the chair against your butt and back, elbows and shoulders. Check to see if the pressure is pleasant or unpleasant in each of these places.

- Take a deep breath, and be aware of the sensations in your throat and chest as you inhale. Let go of the breath. Allow your body to relax and settle in the chair. Take a few more deep breaths and let yourself feel more and more heavy and relaxed.

- Now scan your body for sensations. Slowly move your attention from your scalp down to your toes. Notice any physical feeling, pleasant or unpleasant, as you survey your body.

- Finally, notice your emotional state. Be aware of whether it feels good or bad. Do you want more of this feeling, or would you prefer to escape? Try to attach a label to your emotion—sad, angry, scared, excited, hopeful, happy. Stay with the feeling for a few moments and notice whether it changes.

When you have finished grounding yourself, you'll experience a new sense of calm. As if you were standing on firmer soil. As if you were stronger and straighter and clearer than you felt a few moments before. And there's something else. Your dealings with people will be different now—because you've first listened to the voice of your own body and spirit.

Generosity

Toward the end of his life, Beat poet Kenneth Patchen started writing little four or five line poems for his wife. They described, in the ordinary flow of their days, the extraordinary things he loved about her. They often took no more than ten or twenty minutes to complete, and he wrote a lot of them.

The time Patchen spent creating these little gifts was as nourishing to him as the words of love were to his wife. They were a source both of pleasure and meaning. And he knew, as he wrote them, that they would keep supporting her long after he was gone.

Generosity is self-nourishing. When we take time to give, it usually comes back to us in feelings of worth and a sense of purpose. Not to mention the sweet anticipation of how each generous act can affect others.

A man crafts elaborate and beautiful birdhouses for friends. A woman sews exquisite linings for a baby bassinette each time a family member gets pregnant. Another researches medical questions for friends on the Internet. A mom starts in August to make some really original costumes for her children on Halloween. Another woman pours great creativity into birthdays. The cards she makes for friends are works of art that celebrate what's special and unique about each person.

It doesn't matter what you choose to do or make for others. It doesn't even matter how good you are at it. What's important is the experience of leaving behind your own worries and concerns for a while. Just putting them in the psychological closet while you do something for someone else. The more you lose yourself in the task, the better you feel.

If you'd like to explore generosity as a form of self-nourishment, here are a few ideas to keep in mind:

- **Be specific and simple**. Stay away from complex, multistep tasks.

- **Choose easy activities rather than difficult ones**. Your generosity shouldn't make you feel anxious, or stressed or overwhelmed.

- **Generosity shouldn't be expected or demanded**. It should be something you want to do rather than have to do; obligation takes much of the pleasure out of giving.
- **Don't involve deadlines**. Time pressures can make a gift more of a hassle than anything nourishing.
- **Do things for others that feel rewarding**. Don't research for a friend the best buys in vacuum cleaners if you hate talking to salespeople.
- **Select things that can be done in ten- or fifteen-minute increments.** Something you can pick up quickly, and then put down again with zero fuss.
- **When possible, use your creativity**. Put your own unique stamp on the items you give.
- **Enjoy the good you're doing**. Last, and most importantly, imagine the pleasure each gift or effort will bring. And when you're done, really see the smile on a friend's face. Really hear the thank-you.

Staying with the Flow

Regina parks her car outside the daycare center where her three-year-old is waiting to be picked up. It's 4:52 P.M.; she will shortly walk into the room and he'll rush into her arms. For the moment, though, she sinks into the cushions and takes a deep breath. She lets the air stretch her diaphragm, pushing deep into her abdomen; and when she lets it out her body slumps a little as the muscles relax.

Regina lets her thoughts flow in the moment, focusing on what she feels and sees and hears *right now*. To begin with, she notices that she's tired; her body feels heavy. Emotionally, she notices a sense of relief—as if she had put a burden down.

She takes another deep breath. Regina starts to think of things she has to do next week. Then she catches herself and returns to the moment. Her shoes are tight, yet she notices that her stomach now feels loose and relaxed.

Another deep breath. Someone is shaking a rug out a window across the street; it makes a slight snapping noise. Jewels of light reflect from the hoods and fenders of parked cars. There's a faint smell of sunscreen in the car. For a moment Regina's caught in a mental movie of the sunburn her boy experienced last month. But then she shrugs it off and goes back to the moment.

Another deep breath. And suddenly there's a flash of grief for her dad who passed away last year. Then the loss shifts to affection. Then a mental movie of that birthday when he . . . But she lets go of that too so she can stay here and now. Deep breath.

Another breath. A feeling inside of love for her boy . . . tinged with sadness for a grandpa he'll never remember. And now a sense of calm. Regina notices that the clock reads 5 P.M. She stretches, feeling more centered in herself, and steps out of the car.

What was Regina up to? Regina was doing a centering exercise called "staying with the flow." It helps you relax and feel more aware of yourself. Its effectiveness has been demonstrated by psychological research, and you'll find it easy to learn. Here's what you do:

- Start with a slow, deep breath that stretches and then relaxes your diaphragm.

- Now focus your attention on what's happening *inside* of you at this moment—body sensations as well as emotions. For example, you might notice that your forehead is tight and that you feel a little anxious. Stay with these feelings for a moment; notice if anything changes.

- Take another deep breath and switch your attention to things *outside* of you—sight, sound, smell, and touch. Notice temperature, light and shadow, street sounds, etc.

- Keep switching back and forth between an inner and outer focus. Before each switch, take a deep breath. And always stay in the *now*.

- When you notice yourself slipping into mental movies—scenes from the past (regrets) or projections of the future (worries)—try to steer back to your present experience. Even if you drift into problem solving or planning, try to refocus on the here and now.

- After a while, you may want to stop switching and just flow naturally between your inner and outer experience.

Mental movies cause much of your psychological pain. The more you stay in the flow, the less emotional pain you'll feel. So take a break from the future and the past, from worries, regrets, and problem solving. Stay right here, right now, and feel the centered calmness you can achieve.

Matthew McKay, Ph.D., is the clinical director of Haight Ashbury Psychological Services in San Francisco. McKay is coauthor of 13 popular books, including *The Relaxation & Stress Reduction Workbook, The Daily Relaxer, Self-Esteem, The Self-Esteem Companion,* and *Thoughts & Feelings: The Art of Cognitive Stress Intervention.* In private practice, he specializes in the treatment of anxiety and depression.

Catharine Sutker coauthored *The Self-Esteem Companion* and is a freelance writer living and gardening in Oakland, CA.

Kristin Beck is the coauthor of *Facing 30.* A Seattle-based freelance writer, she's also a dedicated self-nourisher.

Some Other New Harbinger Titles

The Anxiety & Phobia Workbook, 3rd edition, Item PHO3 $19.95

Beyond Anxiety & Phobia, Item BYAP $19.95

The Self-Nourishment Companion, Item SNC $10.95

The Healing Sorrow Workbook, Item HSW $17.95

The Daily Relaxer, Item DALY $12.95

Stop Controlling Me!, Item SCM $13.95

Lift Your Mood Now, Item LYMN $12.95

An End to Panic, 2nd edition, Item END2 $19.95

Serenity to Go, Item STG $12.95

The Depression Workbook, Item DEP $19.95

The OCD Workbook, Item OCD $18.95

The Anger Control Workbook, Item ACWB $17.95

Flying without Fear, Item FLY $14.95

The Shyness & Social Anxiety Workbook, Item SHYW $15.95

The Relaxation & Stress Reduction Workbook, 5th edition, Item RS5 $19.95

Energy Tapping, Item ETAP $14.95

Stop Walking on Eggshells, Item WOE $14.95

Angry All the Time, Item ALL 12.95

Living without Procrastination, Item $12.95

Hypnosis for Change, 3rd edition, Item HYP3 $16.95

Call **toll free, 1-800-748-6273,** or log on to our online bookstore at **www.newharbinger.com** to order. Have your Visa or Mastercard number ready. Or send a check for the titles you want to New Harbinger Publications, Inc., 5674 Shattuck Ave., Oakland, CA 94609. Include $4.50 for the first book and 75¢ for each additional book, to cover shipping and handling. (California residents please include appropriate sales tax.) Allow two to five weeks for delivery.

Prices subject to change without notice.